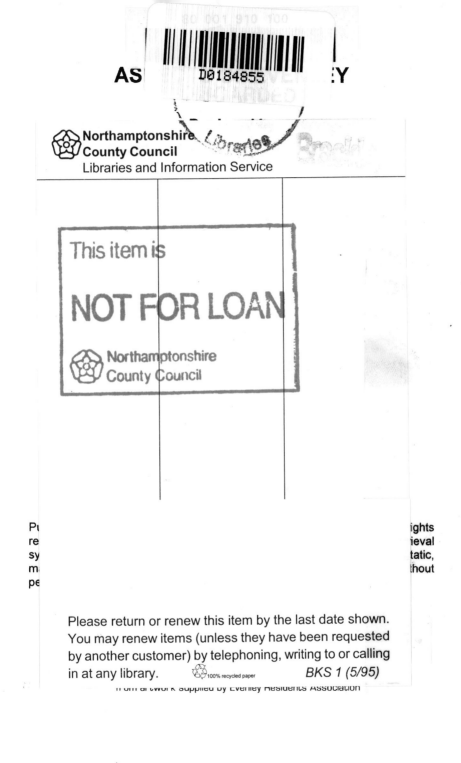

Pı ights
re ieval
sy tatic,
m thout
pe

SPONSORS

We would particularly like to thank our Sponsors for their generous donations which have enabled the publication of this book.

Amors of Evenley
Mike Bosher
Tim Boswell MP
Boots The Chemist
Brackley Antique Cellar
David & Olive Bush
Chris & Marian Chippendale
Jessica Church
Bob & Janet Cropley
Evenley Parish Council
Faccenda Group Ltd
Richard & Ailsa Harris
Jeremy & Josceline Hebblethwaite
Andreas & Philippa Heuman
HFC Consulting
Simon Hollier
Tony & Margaret Hollis
J & C Worldwide Ltd.

Roy & Julia Jennings
Breff & Jill Kelly
Bill & Mae Lacey
Merrick Loggin Trailers
Ian & Liza Moodie
Old Hall Bookshop
Kevin & Carrie O'Regan
John Pepin
Mel & Lee, "The Red Lion"
Brian & Myrtle Robbins
M. Robbins, "Feeling Good Ltd"
Nick Russell & Nick Boffin
The Spencer Family
Tony & Joyce Stevens
Richard & Terry Stopford
Michael & Liz Anne Wainwright
Walford & Round, Brackley
Chris & Emma Wightman

Evenley Cricket Club SNCC Premier League Champions 2001 & 2002

ACKNOWLEDGEMENTS

We would like to thank

1. Les Buggins for permission to quote extracts from his father's book about life in Evenley: 'Life was Like That'.

2. The Spencer family for permission to quote from Mrs Spencer's letter to her grandson.

3. Fox & Sons auctioneers, Bournemouth, for permission to use extracts from the 1938 Evenley Sale Catalogue.

4. The Oxfordshire County Council Photographic Archive for permission to use the photographs of old Evenley from the Packer Collection.

5. The Northamptonshire Record Office for permission to use a photograph of the 1779 Evenley Enclosures Act Map.

6. The Evenley Parish Council for permission to reproduce a copy of The Field Map.

7. Patricia Phillips for the use of the photograph of Thomas Judge's Shop

8. Mr. & Mrs. Chris Wightman for the use of a photograph and details of the history of Evenley Hall.

9. All those who lent photographs for inclusion in the book.

CONTENTS

INTRODUCTION

This is a book about the village and parish of Evenley. It is both a look at how Evenley has developed over time and a look at the village as it is today and how it has been shaped by the past.

We have not been able to write a complete history, because there are long periods where written records are very scarce or non-existent.

Evenley is not a place where great national events occurred, or where famous men and women lived, but it is nevertheless, a place where people have lived and worked for several thousand years. They have not always lived in exactly the same spots, as the archaeological evidence shows us, but through all the changes of cultures, languages and buildings, there has been a community somewhere in the parish for a very long time.

What we offer is some historical background and a series of 'snapshots' of Evenley and its people at particular moments.

We end with a suggested walk around the village as it is now, with notes on buildings of particular interest.

GEOLOGY AND GEOGRAPHY

The parish and village of Evenley lie close to the southern boundary of Northamptonshire, where the County abuts Oxfordshire and Buckinghamshire.

The parish is of irregular shape and covers almost 1300 hectares, including the land of the formerly separate townships of Astwick and Eastwick. The northern boundary of the parish stretches for some distance along the banks of the River Ouse, whilst to the South it reaches Cottisford. Its other boundaries are formed by Mixbury in Oxfordshire on the southeast side, with Tusmore and Croughton to the west.

Near the old mill ford at the bottom of Mill Lane, by the Three Shire Pit, is the point of junction of the parishes of Turweston, Evenley and Mixbury, consequently connecting the three shires, Buckinghamshire, Northamptonshire and Oxfordshire; three dioceses, Lincoln, Peterborough and Oxford; and formerly three legal circuits, Norfolk, Midland and Oxford. Much of this land is a plateau at about 135m, 435 ft, above sea level, with radiating streams, but in the north, the land slopes down to the Great Ouse and its tributary.

On the higher flatter ground, the soil is light loam on thin Eolithic Limestone, perhaps more practically described by the Oxford land agents Dulakes in 1923, as *"variable"*, the Oxfordshire stone brash being much in evidence. It has also been described as *"hungry"* land, having poor producing qualities particularly in unfavourable seasons, with sands and clays exposed on valley sides down to the Ouse.

There is little woodland, but what there is, almost all has been

1

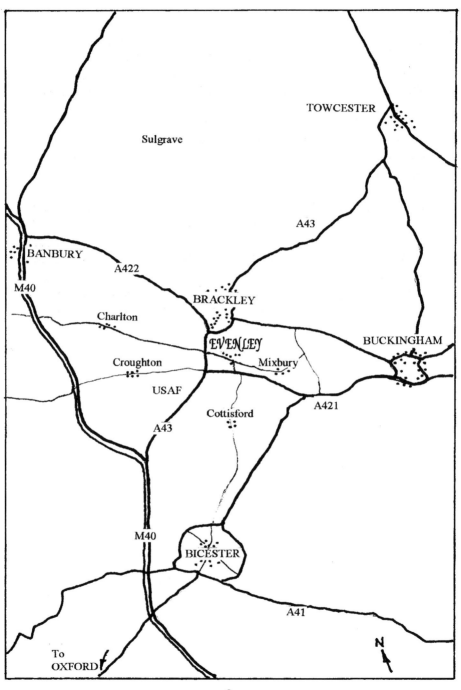

TOWCESTER

Sulgrave

A43

BANBURY

A422

M40

Charlton

BRACKLEY

EVENLEY

BUCKINGHAM

Croughton

Mixbury

USAF

A421

Cottisford

A43

M40

BICESTER

A41

To
OXFORD

N

planted, or re-planted since the Second World War. Former meadows along the Ouse and its tributaries are now, essentially, part of the permanent and semi-permanent pasture which makes up a good proportion of farming land in the parish.

The parish is bisected by the north-south main road the A43, an eleventh century road from Southampton through Oxford to Northampton and by the east-west Buckingham to Chipping Norton road.

Most of the population of around 600 is concentrated in the village of Evenley itself, with smaller hamlets and farmsteads at Bowling Green, Slades Farm, Barley Mow Farm House, Astwick, Plomers Furze Farm, Evenley Lawn Farm, Elm Tree Farm, Evenley Hall and Cloisters Farm. North of the former quarries at Astwick is the site of the deserted village of Eastwick. The Southern boundary of the parish runs close to the USAF base at Croughton.

IMLEY (IMNLEY) – AVELAI –

EVELAI – EVENLEY

Until relatively recently, the village name was Imley and was pronounced as it looks, from the Saxon Imnley - a flat clearing, although it has been suggested that the name may possibly be made up of the two Saxon words, *"eue"* (water) and *"leag"* (pasture). Evenley comes from the written version arising out of the Domesday Book returns, when many Saxon names were francisised. The written version gradually subsumed the original spoken version during the nineteenth century, when incomers brought with them the official version and local people began to use the official version more and more, when dealing with any form of local government; taxes, census, farming returns and postal addresses. Nevertheless, in parish records and on local maps Imley was the preferred spelling, according with local pronunciation, even until the 20th Century.

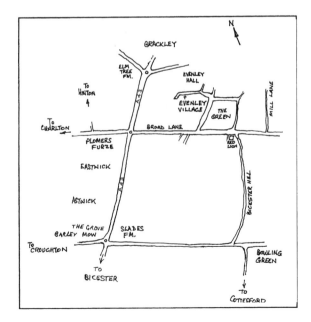

4

PREHISTORIC EVENLEY

With the retreat of the Ice Age around 15,000 BC, prehistoric man gradually re-colonised Britain, moving along river valleys and ridge tops. These people came from what is now Belgium, via the still extant land link to Europe.

The earliest remains found, pinpoint prehistoric settlement in Evenley along the tributaries of the River Ouse in the north of the parish to the west of Mill Lane. The leaf shaped arrow heads, found to the south of the Ouse and west of Mill Lane, are probably Neolithic - 4200 BC to 2100 BC - while 600 yards west along the Ouse, on both banks, is the detritus of a flint working site of the earlier Mesolithic Age.

Flint axe and arrowhead

Finds of pottery sherds indicate that the area has been continuously inhabited. The Great Ouse River would have been an enticement to the Iron Age farmers hoping to settle in this fertile, probably peaceful locality, with its rolling countryside.

There would have been various small farmsteads scattered all along the valley of the river, water being the first requirement to settlement.

The river runs west to east, along the northeast boundary of the village. The river retains its old Celtic name meaning, as far as is known, the *"Ditch of Muddy Water"*.

Many coins and metal objects have been discovered at times when the river has been dredged. These finds would have been items thrown into the river as offerings to the water gods in Celtic and Roman times.

Once the river would have abounded with fish but sadly its water is no longer pure and it is far shallower than it would have been 2000 years ago.

The area, bounded by the Ouse and Addingtons Copse, gives up much Iron Age pottery every ploughing season, which intermingles with Roman pottery and building stone. This suggests that the Romans did not push out the local British Celts in this area, but either lived among them, perhaps as their masters but not separate from them, or the local Celtic lords became Romanised as supportive vassals of the London based Roman state of Britain.

The Celts who lived in the area were the powerful Catuvellauni, who were one of the many Celtic tribes in Britain at this time. The whole of the tribe's area, including Evenley, was under Roman control by AD 44 just a year after Emperor Claudius' army landed on the south coast. We know this from excavations just south of Bicester, which started in 1999. Here was a wooden Roman fort, set in 22 acres, containing a highly mobile garrison of 2,500 men, including archers and horsemen, who acted as a military force against any rebellion in this part of the Midlands and support for the Roman Army at its frontiers. Tree ring dating of well-preserved gatepost timbers put its construction in the Autumn of AD44. There is some evidence that the boundary between the Catuvellauni and the Dobunni to the west, ran along what is now the A43 in this area, the boundary between Evenley and Astwick/Eastwick, which later became a Saxon estate boundary, before being used as the route for the road in the 12th century.

Constantine
(The Great)

Dondius
of Trajan

Sestertius of
Caracalla

Aureus of
Gallienus

ROMAN EVENLEY

It is important to remove preconceptions about Roman Britain. Once the local British, or Celts, had made their peace with the invading army, life went on as before. Local administration and justice would have been overseen by a British official in the Roman British State civil service, based in either

Fragments of Roman Brooch Pins

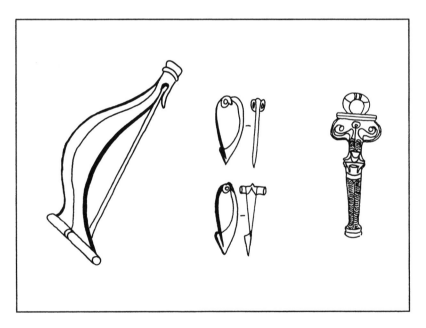

Artist's Impression of Roman Brooch Pins

Towcester or Bicester. Occasionally, army units would pass through on either of the two main roads, between Finmere and the Fosse Way, or Buckingham and Chipping Norton. Perhaps, as a more market – based economy grew out of the mainly subsistence economy, people were able to get hold of more sophisticated goods and wares from further afield, such as higher quality pots and utensils from Gaul and better made plough shares. Coins changed from Celtic to Roman but on the whole life and society changed little.

For most of the Roman occupation the nearest large military post was at Towcester, although archaeological evidence suggests that the Barley Mow site was probably a Roman garrison building at some point during the Roman occupation. While the Roman conquering army was officered by true Romans, the army was largely composed of mercenaries from previously conquered lands of the Roman Empire.

Glass vessel

Roman Glass Sherds from Evenley

9

Only a small proportion of the administrators and civil servants would have been genuine Romans and it would not have been long before others would have been recruited from among the better educated of the native British population. New laws, new currency, new top administrators and new government were gradually imposed, but the people and their ways remained just the same. A good parallel that can be drawn is with that of the British Raj in India.

The main legacy left by the Romans that endured, was the metalled road system and it is now known to be more comprehensive than at first thought. We all know of the main

routes, for they survived to become the basis of our modern trunk road system, e.g. the A5 which was the Roman Watling Street, passing through Towcester. However, there is good evidence for a contributory network of feeder, or cross-country roads, which mainly utilised existing British track ways. One of these almost certainly passed through the middle of Evenley, not the older prehistoric track way from Chipping Norton to Buckingham via the Barley Mow, but what we now know as the Charlton Road - Broad Lane - Mixbury Lane route. This was previously thought to have been mainly set out at the time of the Field Enclosures, two hundred years ago, but a pre-Enclosure map does show this line in use as a by-road and the straightness of the original line is truly Roman. This route linked the Fosse Way through North Oxfordshire and on to Tadmarton, South of Banbury and then, more conjecturally, across the Cherwell near Twyford, through Kings Sutton and eastwards in a straight line through Astrop, Charlton, Evenley, Mixbury and

Finmere, where it met the Roman road from Bicester to Towcester.

There were at least three Roman villas, or farmsteads in Evenley. From the coins, pottery, brick and tile found, we know there was a substantial holding covering many acres, with associated houses and service buildings dating from the first to the 4th century to the north and north-east of Evenley Hall.

Applique vase

Many Roman metal items have been uncovered by responsible metal 'detectorists' and an abundance of Roman pottery pieces represent the whole era of the Roman occupation

Samian Ware found
in the Evenley Area

of Britain. Many pre-Roman Iron Age coins, of more than one British tribe, have also been uncovered hereabouts.

In 1826 in Addingtons meadow, close by the village, a hoard of several hundred Roman coins was found, including some from the reigns of Nero, Domitian, Severus, Constantine and others: the very number of Emperors suggesting a site-life of many generations. Another huge hoard of Roman coins was found in the years before 1854, somewhere to the north of Evenley. A further settlement was to the immediate north of the stream flowing east from Ladybridge and much pottery, building stone and slate is to be found there.

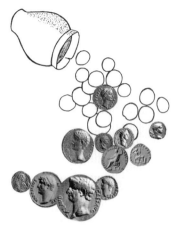

In what is known as the Bury Field, on Plommers Furze, there are scatterings of Roman pottery and a handsome Roman coin is in the possession of the farmer, whose father found it while ploughing in the fifties.

The Roman Hoard

Similarly in Eastwick, there are Roman sherds to be found immediately east of the deserted village, though it is conceivable that this is part of the same settlement at Plommers Furze.

A little pottery of the Roman or Medieval Periods, has been found south of the existing village but one might expect finds at Astwick and Monks House Farm.

Coarse Ware Roman Pottery found locally

Coins were hoarded during times of strife, or when organised trading for money declined into a barter system. Either way it is safe to assume that the Roman administration began to be removed or assimilated back into the native British tribal structure between 250 and 400 AD. The latest Roman coin found at Brackley at the Old Town site, is from 326 AD. Many of the sherds of pottery at the larger Evenley site are of Oxford Ware made at Headington in the second and third century.

The current parish of Evenley had its boundaries finalised by road and stream during this time. It was a place of half a dozen or so prosperous farmsteads, including one that could be described as a villa, stone built with slate roofs. Most labourers lived in thatched huts with timber walls. The modern village was not yet established, but the amount of woodland was probably quite small, about the same as today, concentrated in the south of the Evenley estate. The population would have been over a hundred and all ethnically Celtic as before the Roman occupation.

Roman roof tile sherds
found near Evenley

SAXON EVENLEY AND BEYOND

The local population remained almost unchanged for the next three hundred years before Saxon settlement prevailed upon the area. British tribes were fighting and repulsing Saxon armies at battles such as Stoke Lyne, a few arrow flights to the south, almost into the seventh century.

There may have been ethnic cleansing by the Saxons in the wake of successful military advances into the Celtic west, but it is more likely, given that many Saxons were invited here as mercenaries by the British, that most Saxon settlement in this area followed on the heels of political accommodation with British tribes. There may have been some evictions, from farms and estates, some dispossession of local British lords in favour of Saxon ones, but mass genocide and forced evacuations are unlikely.

The very latest DNA testing techniques are beginning to show that many skeletons found on supposed Saxon sites at many archaeological sites in Middle and South Western England are in fact ethnically Celtic.

Sometime in the eighth or ninth century, the village that became Evenley was formed by the Saxons. If there was a church it was probably wooden. The existing settlements in the west of the current parish were named East Town and West Town - Eastwick and Astwick. The farmstead to the north of the Ladybridge stream continued through this time and Saxon and early medieval pottery, loom weights, querns and coins have been found, while at the Barley Mow site a variety of coins and buckles of the later Medieval period have come to light.

As 'Saxon' England came into being, out of the primary Kingdoms of Mercia, East Anglia, Sussex, Wessex and Kent, the first Royal Edict, concerning local government and taxation, based on the Hundred was issued.

Traditionally, the Hundred was an area supporting a hundred families and belonging to the same great Saxon Lord, usually geographically whole, but sometimes, as with the core part of Evenley, remote from its administrative centre - in this instance Towcester. The overwhelming balance was part of Sutton Hundred, whose administrative centre was at Kings Sutton. This system of taxation, finance and administration was finalised by an edict of King Edgar in 962 AD, by which time the parish of Evenley was largely as now, with hamlets at Evenley, Astwick and Eastwick and farmsteads at Plomers Furze and probably Barley Mow and Bowling Green. The most noticeable manmade feature of the time still exists in part and is the Great Hedge, the "Grosse Haie"; the Saxon Estate Boundary running to the immediate west of what is now the A43.

In the 12thC a stone church was erected by the Lord of the Evenley estate and endowed with lands in the immediate vicinity, probably corresponding with later glebe, or Rectory lands, to the immediate west of the hedge boundary. The church would have been built in line with St Augustine's recommendation, that churches be built on the site of previous pagan worship, but it is not known what lies beneath the foundations The tithes to support the church would have been settled at this time and the parish boundaries already forming the outer frame of the field units becoming fixed for all time. We know from Domesday that the landowners in Evenley, Astwick and Eastwick were two in number – *Leofnoth* and *Leofstan* and that the latter was probably the church benefactor. Otbert, a Saxon, who was the local tenant at Domesday, probably lived locally and sub-let to individual farmers. He was not affected when Leofnoth and Leofstan, or their heirs, lost their land to Norman magnates.

The Green did not exist and was not to do so as common property for nearly nine hundred years after Domesday. The village of Imley (as it was pronounced by the locals), was gathered around the church at the end of Church Lane. The expansion towards the east, along Church Lane, happened during medieval times and much medieval pottery has been found in the gardens of the modern houses on both sides of the lane

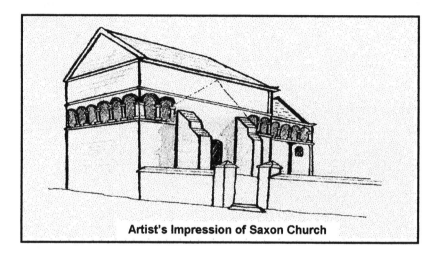

Artist's Impression of Saxon Church

The medieval church occupied the same site as the present one and just to the east of it lay a moated manor house. The remains of the moat can be seen quite clearly on the Enclosure map of 1779 and parts of it are visible on OS maps from the first half of last century. The oldest part of Rectory Farm already existed and was a building belonging to the Abbey of St. Mary in Huntingdon, who also held the advowson of the Church. Other religious houses that owned land in Evenley were St. John's Hospital in Brackley and De La Pré Abbey in Northampton.

Away from the village houses, the original medieval fishpond lay near to what is now Bicester Hill. There was probably a windmill to the northwest of the village and according to the Domesday Book there were four water mills in Evenley in 1086. There was still a mill on the Ouse at the end of Mill Lane in 1779.

Who would have owned the manor? Nowadays, we tend to think of a house when we use the word *"manor"*, but actually, a manor was a holding of land that included rights to collect various dues, either in money, or in kind. If there was a manor house, it was not necessarily lived in by the Lord of the Manor and the land was often let out to tenants. It looks as if at some periods there was more than one manor in Evenley and these are sometimes described by the name of the family holding them at the time. For instance, there is a record of a *"Gawlton's Manor"* in the 16th century. One man, who was certainly in possession of the *"Manor of Evenley"*, was William de Apeltree, who founded a chantry in the church in the fourteenth century.

Evenley's great moment came at the end of the 12th century, when one of only five licensed tournament fields in the whole of England was established here. In the eleven hundreds, tournaments were huge melees of armed horsemen, like two rival armies, ranging over a mile or two of open countryside. There was often considerable loss of life and the whole thing tended to degenerate into a general riot. In an effort to control things, Richard I (Richard the Lionheart) designated five places where tournaments could legally be held and then only by licence. One of these was in Evenley, although it is often described in old texts as being at Brackley, or *"between Brackley and Mixbury"*. It is in fact recorded as being at Bayards Green, which was the name for the flat land now on either side of the B4031 road from the Barley Mow to Buckingham.

The foundations of three small buildings from the later Saxon period have been uncovered in the area known as "The Grove", which lies to the immediate north of the Barley Mow and there is some evidence of this ground being cultivated as a garden by a Mr. Gosforth in 1275. There also existed two stew ponds that were listed ancient monuments at one time, but these have been completely obliterated by subsequent farming, as have the "hollow ways", the Saxon track ways which connected the various hamlets and farms.

In 1425 there is evidence to suggest that the Barley Mow was a large and thriving hostelry and it continued as an Inn until the early part of last century. The foundations of the building also suggest that at some time in its history it acted as a changing station for coach horses.

After the dissolution of the monasteries in the 16th century, the land and advowson belonging to Huntingdon Priory were bought by Sir Thomas Pope, a speculator originally from Banbury who went on to found Trinity College, Oxford. He sold the Evenley land off very quickly and it was later bought by the Master of Magdalen College, Oxford, which already owned all the former St. John's Hospital land in Brackley and Evenley. Thereafter, the two major landowners in Evenley were Magdalen College and the Lord of the Manor, a situation that was to last for more than 350 years.

The Lisle family of Brackley bought the Lordship of the Manor of Evenley from the Stutesbury family in the late 16th century. The Lisles were yeoman farmers, who were going up in the world and they had reached gentry status by 1604, when William Lisle was MP for Brackley. William wanted very much to be accepted socially and claimed to be a descendent of quite a prestigious medieval family of Lisles, whose arms he unsuccessfully tried to assume. The Lisles moved to Evenley some time before 1666 and would have lived in what was then the new Manor House, which we call the Old Manor and which had replaced the old moated one. The family fortunes were declining by the end of the century, though a Toby Lisle, who was a captain in the Navy, managed to restore them briefly later, with substantial prize money gained fighting the French in the West Indies. He married a wealthy widow with a large estate on the island of Antigua, but was killed in a duel in 1719. He left the Antigua estate to his nephew Fermor Lisle, who was by now the head of the family in Evenley and Fermor was able to live in a very grand manner for a while on the income.

Fermor's younger brother, another William, had already been sent out to Antigua to help run the plantation, mainly to get him away from a servant girl he had offered to marry. However, William was unsuccessful as a plantation manager and in any case he died young in 1731. No other family member could be persuaded to go out to Antigua, so the plantation was left in the hands of local managers. When Fermor died in 1742, it was discovered that he had been financing his expensive lifestyle by borrowing heavily against the security of the Antigua estate and had in fact borrowed far more than its actual value. Both the Antigua and Evenley estates had to be sold. Some of the Lisle memorials can still be seen in the church.

Another important family in the village during the same period were the Levinzes, originally from Westmoreland, who were tenants of Magdalen College at Rectory Farm for several generations. The most famous member of the family was Sir Creswell Levinz, who was a distinguished lawyer, judge and Attorney General for a time, during the reign of Charles II. He published two influential books on case law, one in French and one in Latin. His tomb is the flamboyant, though sadly deteriorating one, in the churchyard, to the north of the chancel. The figure from his memorial is still in the church. The memorial was originally very large and was on the chancel wall. Creswell's younger brother, Baptista Levinz, became Bishop of Sodor and Man.

After the decline of the Lisles, the manor of Evenley was sold to one William Price, Esquire and then following his death it was purchased by Francis Basset, of Tehidy in Cornwall. He was a younger son and doubtless wanted to establish his own estate. He built the present Evenley Hall, although what we see today is largely the result of extensive rebuilding following a fire at the end of the 19th century. He also managed to enclose substantial land around the Hall for gardens and parkland, including a deer park. Most of the agricultural land in the parish was still being farmed in three large open fields, as it had been since medieval times, but in 1779, the major local landowners succeeded in obtaining a Parliamentary act allowing them to enclose the open fields and redistribute them in convenient blocks. This was done in 1780. The enclosure would have had a dramatic effect on the appearance of the landscape, as all the new fields had to be fenced and hedged, the roads were straightened and farmers began to build new farmhouses away from the village among their own fields. The enclosure greatly benefited the Vicar and a fine new vicarage was completed in Broad Lane in 1834.

The main road, the A43, which bisects the parish on a north

Artist's impression of a tollgate

south alignment was laid out in the 100 years following the conquest, in order to provide a speedy route between Winchester and Southampton and the north via Northampton. In this parish, it was adjacent to the Saxon boundary hedge on its west side and Barley Mow. The double formation of this ancient hedge becomes more apparent, when one compares it to normal enclosure type field hedges, where the individual hawthorns lie in crocodile file; here they are three and four abreast. The road was *'turnpiked'* in the nineteenth century and there was a building called Knights House, which was probably a Tollgate House on the county border. The road was tarmacadamed only after the first world war and used by Flora Thompson's father every day on his way to work in Brackley (see Lark Rise to Candelford by Flora Thompson) and is mentioned for being very white and dusty in the summer months.

"Comparing the time of which I write to the present day, what changes there have been! From travel on foot, horse and train to travel to the moon. Surely, no generation has been in such a position before to witness so much change in such a short time."

Life was Like That – 1976 – W. Buggins

MEDIEVAL EVENLEY

There are not many individuals, who emerge from the medieval history of Evenley, but we do know a little about two men who were farming here in the fifteenth century. William Sawter died here in 1469 and Thomas Smalbon in 1500 and the probate copies of both their wills are in the collection of the Northamptonshire County Records Office. They give a tantalisingly brief glimpse of their world.

Medieval wills follow a definite pattern, usually beginning with a declaration that the testator is of sound mind, then dealing in turn with the disposal of the soul and the body before passing on to individual bequests. Most wills were written when death was thought to be imminent, or at least a strong possibility, for instance, when setting out on a military campaign. Witnesses were unnecessary if the will was written in the testator's own hand, although the parish priest was often present and indeed this was considered one of his pastoral duties, particularly in the case of a death-bed will. This may account for the frequent small bequests to the local vicar that appear. Wills were governed by Church law and had to be examined by the Bishop, or his officer, who granted probate, if they were found to be genuine. He had the power to appoint executors, if the testator had not done so. Wills of this period could be written in either English or Latin. Both of these are in Latin. In the fifteenth century, wills only dealt with personal property, animate or inanimate and not with land, so we cannot tell how much land either of them might have owned. However, they both seem to have been farming in a reasonably substantial way. The wills have been translated into English and some punctuation added to make them easier to read, as there was effectively no punctuation used at the time they were written. The spellings of place and family names have been left exactly as they appear in the originals, although any Latinised Christian names have been given their most common English equivalents, for instance,

"Joan" for *"Johana"* and *"Roger"* for *"Rogerus"*. It is interesting to see that in both wills, *"Evenley"* is spelt exactly as it is today. This could easily not have been the case, as spelling was still very fluid at this period and it is quite usual to find three or four different spellings of the same place, or person, in one document.

Both wills are quite short and it is disappointing that they do not make any reference to personal possessions. Apart from money bequests, both men are primarily disposing of their animals. They are probably assuming that their nearest relatives, a wife in the case of William and a brother in the case of Thomas, will have their personal belongings. Here is William Sawter's will of 1469.

"Anno domini MCCCCLxix

In the name of God, Amen. On the twenty-fourth day of the month of November AD 1469 I, William Sawter of Evenley, being of sound mind and good memory, make my testament in this way. First I leave my soul to Almighty God, to the blessed Mary and to all the saints and my body to be buried in the chancel of the parish church of St. George at Evenley.

Item, I bequeath to the high altar of the said church four ells of linen cloth. Item, I bequeath to the aforesaid church a large bell. Item, I bequeath for the repair of the bell tower 20 of the best of all my rams. Item, I bequeath for a priest to celebrate Mass for the salvation of my soul and the souls of my friends for one year in the aforesaid church eight marks. Item, I bequeath to Joan my daughter 10 breeding ewes. Item, I bequeath to Anne my daughter 40 breeding ewes. Item, I bequeath to Isabel, Anne's daughter, 20 sheep. Item, I bequeath to Joan Wattis ten sheep. Item, I bequeath to Eleanor Ball 4 sheep. Item, I bequeath to John Wattis 4 sheep. Item, I bequeath to John Skylman two sheep.

The rest of my goods not already bequeathed, I give and bequeath to Edmund Thorne, to Sir Roger Morley the chaplain and to Joan my wife, who I appoint my true executors, to dispose of for the good of my soul".

Probate was granted on the 19th of December, so William could not have lived long after writing his will. A mark, a common unit of currency, was 13s.4d. and an ell was 1¼ yards when applied to cloth. Roger Morley was indeed the Vicar of Evenley at the time and his name can be seen on the list in the church. The *"sir"* is simply a courtesy title customarily given to priests and does not mean he was a knight or baronet.

Thomas Smalbon's will of 1500, reads:-

"In the name of God, Amen. Anno domini one thousand five hundred, I Thomas Smalbon make my testament in this way. First I bequeath my soul to Almighty God and my body to be buried in the church of St. George at Evenley. Item, I bequeath to that church 6s.8d. for my burial. Item, to the mother church of Lincoln 20d. Item, to the church of Eydon 40d. Item, to the church of Hynton two breeding ewes. Item, to the church of Mixbery 16d. Item, to John Smalbon two oxen and 20 sheep. Item, I bequeath to Henry Smalbon 20 sheep. Item, to John Moll 20 sheep. Item, to Lucy Moll one cow and ten breeding ewes. Item, to William Moll ten sheep. Item, to Alice Moll ten sheep. Item, to the Vicar of Evenley 20d.

The rest of my goods not bequeathed as above I give and bequeath to John Smalbon my brother, whom I appoint my executor, to dispose of for the good of my soul".

Probate was granted on the 27th of May 1500. The *"mother church of Lincoln"* is Lincoln Cathedral, as all of this area was in the diocese of Lincoln, until the creation of the diocese of Peterborough in 1541.

The phrase *"To dispose of for the good of my soul"* at the end of both wills is more than just a pious platitude. The aim was to reduce the length of time the soul would spend in Purgatory, which could be done by means of requiem masses (as William Sawter provides for in his will), by the prayers of priests, monks, nuns or the poor which would all have to be paid for and by deeds of charity done in the name of the deceased.

One can only speculate as to what Evenley would have been like at this time. Most of the land around the village was farmed in open fields for growing crops, but it is obvious from the number of sheep mentioned in the two wills that sheep farming was also a significant activity. The eighteenth-century map of the parish shows old enclosures along the river and its tributary, as well as shared meadowland and these may have been used for sheep. Brackley had been a wool town since the thirteenth century and provided a market for wool produced in the surrounding area, although it was never as important, or profitable, as some of the Cotswold wool towns. Much of the local wool was sent to London via Buckingham, Brickhill and Dunstable and was shipped to Flanders for processing.

"Most farms had their flocks of sheep and in some cases father and son were shepherds. The wages and hours were much the same for these as the carters and stockmen. The sheep were penned on the ploughland, feeding on mustard, turnips, kale, hay and swedes throughout the winter months. They got very dirty and in April and May were driven in flocks across the Green on their way down to Washbrook at the New Pond where they were washed ready for shearing during the month of May."

Life was Like That – 1976 – W. Buggins

THE CIVIL WAR

Half of the military action in the first English Civil War, (1642 - 1646), took place in the Midlands. The Royal capital at Oxford twenty miles away and the Parliamentarian capital in London seventy miles away, dictated that most of the strategic manoeuvring should take place between the two. Two main routes used by both sides armies and local troops were the Oxford to Northampton road and the Buckingham to Chipping Norton road, both of which run through the parish and intersect at the then Barley Mow inn. The closest garrisons were the Royalist capital and its perimeter garrison at Banbury, while Northampton was staunchly Parliamentarian throughout the war.

Fighting had started in the summer of 1642 and on The 22nd of August 1642, three Troops of Horse were sent from Nottingham to Oxford, under the command of Sir John Byron, to convoy a large sum of money and valuables for the King's cause. On Sunday the 28th, as the Royalists halted in Brackley for supper, they were attacked by a force of 500 Northampton men. Most of the Cavaliers escaped toward Evenley on the main road, apart from 60 or 70 men and their horses, which were taken. The captives were taken prisoner to the garrison at Northampton, while their horses were distributed among the locals, after the Roundheads took the best for re-mounts. Worse than this for the Cavaliers, *"two hatfuls of gold, about 2,000 pounds in silver, a trumpet, a box with great riches and wealth; a packet of rich cloaths of Sir John Byron's worth 200 pounds; about fourteen or fifteen pair of pistols; a sumpter horse of Sir John Bryon's, very rich and betwixt 60 or 70 men were taken. The value of all the gold, money and apparel could not be worth less than 6 or 8,000 pounds! As for the horses whatsoever any particular man that tooke, he hath it to himself, insomuch that many of the men have gotten them horses and ride home on them. Two of the cavaliers were hidden overnight by two sympathisers and conveyed out of Brackley early next day. They were chased and caught in Evenley's Brackley field, probably near Ladybridge, two of our company got each of them a sword and I searching under one of their coats, found a pistol charge with a brace of bullets, which I took from him and that I keep. One of Byron's men, entrusted with a cabinet, a packet of writings and other things of great value, got lost and hid the items in an oat field near Pimlico House. He was eventually arrested by Mr Clarke and the village constable in Croughton. He was forced to 'discover all' to soldiers of the Banbury garrison".*

On January 22nd 1643, Prince Rupert himself was with his army in and around Brackley, scouring the bountiful Parliamentary countryside and villages for re-mounts. He wrote to Henry Hastings in Ashby de la Zouch. *"At ten in the morning. Brackley. - By reason that there are above 400 of our musketeers unmounted, we shall be a day later, but upon Thursday expect us about Lester and if possible get horses to meet us for our men and I pray send an express to my Lord Newcastell to let him know so much. In the meanwhile send me all the intelligence you have of the rebels moving and I shall he very ready to follow your counsel in anything." Signed, Rupert.*

On May 6th 1643, there was nearby action at Middleton Cheney when the Earl of Northampton's Banbury Royalists fought with the Parliamentary Northampton forces, slaying about 200 of them and taking 300 prisoners with much ordnance. Later in the summer, Sir John Byron's troop had its revenge over the local militia, when 200 Northampton men were surprised on the Bicester road and a number of men were killed, including a captain. For most of the war, there was a Royalist outpost of sixty men in the great house at Aynho and the regular carriers went no further south than Brackley; any military supplies moving south or east-west through the parish went with heavy escorts.

Apart from movement of the great armies along the two main roads and innumerable smaller troop movements, Evenley was in the front line for most of the war between the Parliamentarian garrison at Newport Pagnell and the Royalists at Oxford and Banbury. Larger parties from each, would occasionally ambush smaller parties from each, on the two great roads through the parish. Once a troop of Parliamentary Horse ambushed a Royalist party somewhere near Astwick, a mile west of Evenley and carried off oxen they had probably rustled themselves. One of the luckless Royalists wrote back to Banbury from jail in Newport Pagnell, " *it was our hard chance to be taken prisoner between Aynho and Brackley, a coast where I little dreamed of danger, which came unlooked for and since Fate hath brought us into durance at Newport I hope your worship will afford us exchange from Banbury, or be pleased to send us some monyes for our subsistence until a happy exchange may bee sent*".

In August 1643, the Earl of Essex and a large force had reached Brackley from Bicester and camped on Brackley Heath. On September 1st, joined by the London Trained Bands and militia, he left Brackley over the Ouse Bridge and marched along the main road through the parish all the while shouting and waving at the credulous rustics lining the roadside, thence to the Barley Mow where he turned for Chipping Norton and eventually the relief of Gloucester. During that last week in August, the Parliamentary committee in Northampton would have ensured that in Evenley, like other villages close to Brackley, the ordinary soldiers were billeted four to a cottage and the officers and "gentlemen of quality" quartered in the farmhouses and manor house. Two months later, there was a Royalist upsurge in the district. On 6th October, Newport Pagnell was captured by Colonel Dyve for the King, but owing to a communications breakdown, reinforcements were too late and the town had to be abandoned, much to Prince Rupert' s chagrin on October 27th. He tried to fortify Towcester during November and supplies from Oxford were constantly convoyed to that place through Evenley, sometimes under the personal supervision of the Prince himself. However, the risk to the convoys from the

Northampton militia once they passed Baynards Green, was eventually found to be too great and reluctantly Rupert abandoned the project.

In March 1644, the Royalist outpost at Hillenden House near Buckingham fell to the Parliamentarians and Cromwell himself had his headquarters in Buckingham for a short while. By June 1644, Charles 1st himself was at Buckingham with his main army, prior to moving northwest along the banks of the Ouse toward Brackley and Evenley and thence to the battle at Cropredy Bridge, where he defeated Waller.

A year later, the roads through South Northamptonshire were clogged with fleeing Royalists making their sorry way to Oxford, after their shattering defeat at Naseby. Never again were the local people to see any great armies on the move, until the preparations for D-Day exactly a year short of three hundred years later, when the Northampton-Oxford road was jammed with armoured vehicles and trucks making for Southampton and Portsmouth. Of local people's attitudes to the civil war, we know nothing for certain, although we may surmise that the Levinzes at Rectory Farm, with their Magdalen College connection and the Lisles at the Manor House, with their enthusiastic attitude to things noble and royal, would have been sympathetic at the very least to the Royalist cause. Rather surprisingly in 1649, the vicar of Evenley, Timothy Perkins, was bold enough to sign his name to a local petition to the Lord Fairfax in London, protesting against the trial of the King.

THE EVENLEY ENCLOSURE OF 1780

In the latter half of the eighteenth century, Evenley, like many parishes in Northamptonshire, was still being farmed under the common (or open) field system that had been used for centuries. Of 315 parishes in the County, less than 100 were enclosed by 1765. The basic unit of the common field system was the strip, a long, narrow piece of land, which varied greatly in size from place to place. Strips running in the same direction were grouped together in furlongs and the furlongs in turn into two or three very large arable fields. The method of ploughing used always threw the soil off the ploughshare toward the centre of the strip, resulting in the soil of the strip building up into a high ridge, separated from the next strip by a narrow, much lower section of unploughed land, which also acted as drainage. This ridged pattern can still be seen today in fields that have not been ploughed in recent times. The rest of the land was made up of grassland for grazing and *"common"*, or *"waste"*, uncultivated land, or woodland which could be used as extra pasturage and for the collection of firewood or other fuel.

Individual landowners would have a number of strips in different parts of each field, so that the better and worse land was shared out fairly.

There were no hedges or fences between the strips or furlongs and cultivation was organised on a communal basis and controlled by a Manor Court, made up of representatives of the landowners. They decided on the crops to be sown in each field and on the dates of opening and closing the common pastureland. Land would be left fallow in rotation, which

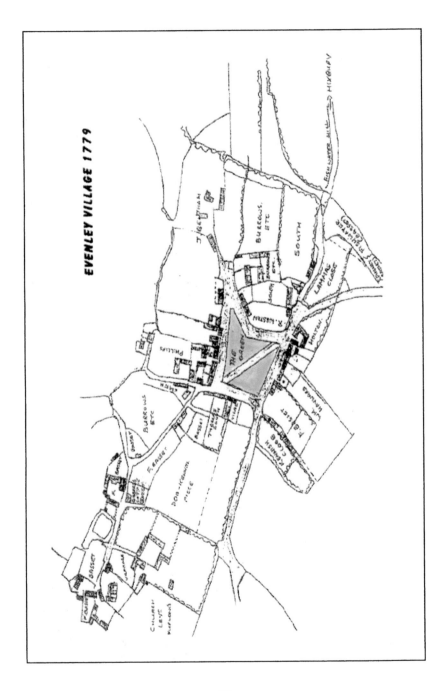

EVENLEY VILLAGE 1779

provided extra grazing for stock and a chance for the land to recover fertility. It was a cumbersome system, but one in which all but the very poorest had some rights in the common fields and lands, enabling most families to support themselves. Those with no rights over the arable land often had grazing rights, so that they could keep a cow, pigs, or geese and they could gather fuel on the common waste. In this area, the fuel source was predominantly furze.

In Evenley before its enclosure, there were three open fields, the Brackley Field to the west, the Middle Field to the south and the Mill Field to the east. There were also areas of meadowland and pasture near the river and a waste known as Cotisford Heath along the Buckingham road.

Of course, there had always been pressure from powerful landowners to enclose the common land for their own use and in some parts of the country, this had occurred much earlier. In Evenley, there were enclosed areas to the north of the village along the River Ouse and its tributary, which form the boundary between the village and Brackley. These areas of land belonged to the Lord of the Manor, Francis Basset of Evenley Hall and to Magdalen College, the vicarages of Brackley and Hinton and to some individuals. Francis Basset had provoked something of a riot in 1758 by enclosing some land on the Heath for game. There is a letter in the archive of Magdalen College from their steward, a Mr. Barton, who had been asked to report on the situation. As the major landowner in Evenley, the College felt it ought to keep an eye on things. Mr. Barton reported that Mr. Basset had enclosed three to four acres of furze land and *"the poor people having usually cut furze upon it looked upon it as an encroachment of their privileges"*. He was careful to add that the poor had no legal right to cut furze, but had only customarily done so. The poor had then assembled *"in a rude and disorderly manner"* and *"have proceeded to several outrages as cutting down of young trees and such things to show their resentment"*. They tore down Mr. Basset's fences and destroyed the furze. Mr. Basset had threatened that if he were to be obstructed in his enclosure, he would enclose a hundred acres the next year *"or bring on a parcel of sheep"*. He was brought before the Manor Court, but seems to have had his own his way.

The action of the poor on this occasion was quite usual. The prospect of an enclosure often brought riots, particularly in the Midlands and the South. There was a particularly violent one in West Haddon in 1765, which grew out of a football match, possibly planned as a cover for the subsequent attack on the newly-erected fences. It was reported in the *"Northampton Mercury"* of 5th August of that year and a party of Dragoons had to be sent to apprehend the rioters. Even for those with actual legal rights in the land, enclosure could be ruinous. The expenses of enclosure, where each proprietor had to pay a proportion of the cost and be responsible for the fencing of his new fields were such that those with only small amounts of land could often not afford to take them up and had to sell them to larger landowners.

Mr. Basset's enclosure was but a first step. There was a growing movement across the country for wholesale enclosure in the name of agricultural improvement. The eighteenth century saw a revolution in agricultural methods, as it did in manufacturing and these were almost impossible to implement under an open field system. There were also very large profits to be made by landowners, who could see the rental value of their land increase three or four times. The Church too benefited, as tithe payments were usually converted into grants of land. Enclosure also fitted well with the philosophical temper of the times, which valued rationality and order above all things. There were even moral arguments to be deployed. Several commentators noted how difficult it was for landowners to ensure they had sufficient paid labourers under the common field system, as the commoners frequently had other things to do than work for the landowner. Enclosure was seen as a powerful force for social control, as in the *"Report on Shropshire for the Board of Agriculture"* of 1794, where the author points out, that *"the use of Common Land by labourers operates upon the mind as a sort of independence"*.

After enclosure, on the contrary, *"the labourers will work every day in the year, their children will be put out to labour early"* and *"that subordination of the lower ranks of Society which in the present times is so much wanted, would be thereby considerably served"*.

From about 1760, Acts of Parliament to enclose villages became increasingly frequent. The procedure was to present a petition from a group of local people, which could be done quite secretly until 1774, when Parliament decreed that notice of the petition must be displayed on the church door for three Sundays in August or September. The petition would almost certainly result in the petitioners being given leave to present a Bill, which would in due course become an Act enabling the enclosure. Protests from small landowners were unlikely to have much effect, even if they could afford to be represented.

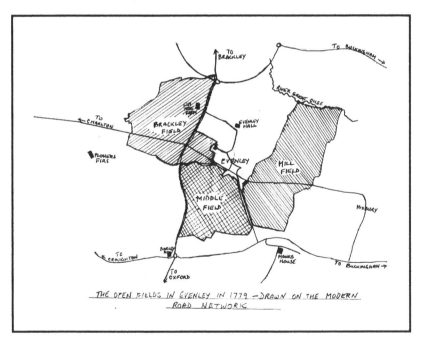

THE OPEN FIELDS IN EVENLEY IN 1779 - DRAWN ON THE MODERN ROAD NETWORK

35

"An Act for Dividing and Inclosing the Open Common Field and Commonable Lands and Grounds, within the Manor and Parish of Evenly, otherwise Bury Manor, in the County of Northampton" was passed in 1779. The persons named in the Act as local landowners are likely to have been its main sponsors. They are Francis Basset, Esquire (Lord of the Manor), who was the son of the Francis Basset enclosing land on the Heath in 1758, the President and Scholars of Saint Mary Magdalen College, Oxford (also patrons of the vicarage and parish Church, sharing the right of appointing the vicar with the Lord of the Manor and owners of the rectory and parsonage lands), the Reverend John Finden (Vicar), the Duke of Bridgewater, Jeremiah Bentham, Esquire, Joseph Painter *"and divers others"*. Obtaining the Act of Parliament must have been expensive and the costs of the enclosure would also have been considerable.

The Act named two Commissioners to oversee the enclosure, one of whom, Robert Weston, was Land Agent to the Cartwrights at Aynho and was himself the lessee of some of the College's land in Evenley and Astwick. It also specified three *"Quality Men"* to undertake a valuation of all the land by the 1st of August 1779, or as soon after as was possible and two Surveyors to make a full survey before the 1st of October that year, or as soon after as could be done. The survey was to show the number of acres, roods and perches belonging to each proprietor, together with the value of each holding. In the event of any dispute arising over current rights in the land, or in the shares to be allocated under the eventual enclosure, the Commissioners were authorised to assess the evidence by examining witnesses under oath and the decisions they reached would be binding on all parties. However, anyone who felt that they had been unjustly treated could take the matter to law.

In the meantime, the Commissioners were to take over the function of the Manor Court, deciding what land could be stocked with cattle, what crops should be sown (though no meadowland was to be ploughed up before the enclosure was completed) and they were further given the power to *"suspend or totally extinguish all or any part of the right of common in and over the said lands and grounds intended to be inclosed"*, by displaying a notice to that effect on the church door in Evenley. Any cattle put out to pasture after the rights of common were extinguished would be impounded and would be returned to the owner only on the payment of 2 shillings per beast.

The Commissioners were also to lay out both public and private roads and were to set aside land, not to exceed two acres in total, for public stone pits, in order to provide material for the repair of such roads; they were to set aside land to the yearly value of ten pounds, which sum was to be used to compensate the poor of the parish for the loss of the *"usage"* of cutting furze. The land was to be allotted to the Vicar, Churchwardens and Overseers of the Poor and the income to be used for the benefit *"of the most necessitous, industrious and honest poor inhabitants of the said parish, who shall not be provided for in the Poor House of the said parish"*. The income was to be distributed on the 21st of December each year in the form of either money or fuel.

The Act went on to specify all aspects of the coming enclosure, including the fees to be paid to the Commissioners, £1.11s.6d. per day each, plus expenses. The Vicar, as lessee of Magdalen College, was to receive one fifth in value of all the arable land and one ninth of all the meadow and pasture land, in lieu of several types of tithes previously paid by landholders. Other tithes and glebe rights were to be exchanged for further land and some tithes were replaced by quarterly payments. Allotments of land were to be fenced by the new proprietors within twelve months of the award, apart from most of the Vicar's land, which was to be fenced at the expense of the other proprietors.

A period of six months was allowed for the previous owners to take away any trees, hedges, bushes, furze or shrubs, provided they made good the ground by levelling it afterwards and gaps were to be left in the fences for twelve months, to allow the passage of cattle or vehicles. No lambs were to be kept for four years, as they might damage fencing, or newly planted hedges. Any proprietor failing to fence his allotment would have it fenced by the Commissioners, who would then be legally empowered to recover the cost from him. There was also a clause allowing proprietors to exchange allotments, if it seemed more convenient to them.

The Commissioners were bound to hold public meetings, so that any objections to their proposals could be raised. Unfortunately, no records of the meetings, or of the deliberations of the Commissioners, Quality Men and Surveyors have survived, but we do have two most important documents, the map drawn for the original survey and a copy of the final Award.

The map, which may be seen in the County Records Office at Wooton Hall, Northampton, is a fascinating record of the village as it was in 1779.

It excludes Astwick, which belonged wholly to Magdalen College and was already enclosed, although a few details such as the buildings at Barley Mow, are sketched in. The Map is in four large separate sheets and shows the old furlongs of the open fields (though not, unfortunately, their owners) and the old enclosures, many of which do have names attached. Later, someone has drawn in the boundaries of the redistributed holdings in a different ink, which is markedly more faded than the original, but can usually be made out. Sometimes the name of the new owner has been written in. Apart from Evenley Hall and the Mill, which can be seen on the Ouse with its millpond and race at the top of Mill Lane, there are very few buildings to be seen beyond the confines of the actual village. It was only after enclosure that farmhouses were built outside the village, surrounded by their fields.

The Parish Council is fortunate in owning a copy of the Enclosure Award, which was enrolled in Northampton on 1st August 1781.

The process had been completed in the spring of 1780 and the Award was signed by the Commissioners at a public meeting held in the Crown at Brackley on the 23rd March. They reported that the three Quality Men had made a *"valuation quality and appraisement of the said lands and grounds and also of the old inclosed lands within the said Parish of Evenly which were intended to be exonerated from tithes or exchanged"* and that *"the same was reduced into writing and signed by all the said Quality Men and after was open to the inspection of all and every of the proprietors interested in the said enclosure...at the several subsequent meetings of us the Commissioners and such objections as were made thereto were upon a review settled and determined."* It adds that the Commissioners, *"having well considered such survey and admeasurements and often viewed the said open common field and commonable grounds ... and also the old enclosure intended to be exonerated from tithes or exchanged .... (have) heard and duly informed ourselves of the rights and claims of all parties interested therein and settled and determined the same and all disputes and differences between the said parties".* They had set out all the public roads and ways that were to pass over the land and heard and dealt with all objections to these at a public meeting held at the house of William Walton (Barley Mow) on 16th August 1779. The Award goes on to list in detail all the allotments made, a total of 1,444 acres 3 roods and 6 perches, including roads and track ways. There are four roods in an acre and forty perches in a rood.

The preamble to the Award features a slightly different list of landowners from that in the Act. This time, they are given as Sir Francis Basset (by now a baronet and later Lord de Dunstanville and Stratton), the President and Scholars of Saint Mary Magdalen College Oxford, the Reverend John Finden, John Burrows, Gentleman, George Thomas, Gentleman, Mary Davis, Widow, Ann Davis, Spinster, John Stevens, Gentleman (as guardian for Ann Burrows, a minor) and Thomas Hopcraft. Thomas Hopcraft was a Churchwarden at the time and his name is spelt *"Hopcroft"* throughout, although it has in some places had the *"o"* changed to an *"a"* later and the transcription of his signature at the end of the document certainly has an *"a"*, so this is likely to have been how he spelt it.

Of those who sponsored the Act, or who are named in the preamble to the Award, several were given rather modest allotments and were presumably named because of their social position rather than because they were large landowners in Evenley. The Duke of Bridgewater, for instance, only received 5 acres 1 rood and 6 perches. Mary Davis was allotted two small plots in the village totalling 6 acres 2 roods, 24 perches, while Ann Davis, described as *"spinster"* and perhaps Mary's daughter or sister-in-law received 8 acres and 18 perches. It is interesting to see that Ann Davis was the only one of those named in the preamble to have been unable to sign her name at the end of the document; she is represented by *"Ann Davis, her mark"*.

The total land allotted to John Finden in his various capacities as lessee of the College, as Vicar, in lieu of different types of tithes and in lieu of glebe lands, comes to 449 acres and 23 perches in two distinct blocks, one around Broad Lane with another two fields to the south of the Charlton road and the other to the west of Mill Lane. Sir Francis Basset received 251 acres and 14 perches in the village and to the west of the Oxford Road, including the Village Green.

Jeremiah Bentham, Esquire, who already had old enclosures to the northeast of the village, was allotted 98 acres and 21 perches adjoining them in right of his wife and purchased the rights to a further 5 acres 2 roods and 14 perches from Joseph Haynes. A Joseph Haynes had sold the Manor in Evenley in 1716. He would have been very old by 1780, so this Joseph, probably belongs to a later generation. John Burrows and John Stevens, styled *"Gentlemen"*, each held one-third shares in the same pieces of land, Stevens holding his as the guardian of Ann Burrows, who was a minor. John Burrows increased his share by purchasing the rights to the final third from a Richard Kerby and his wife,

40

Elizabeth. George Thomas, also styled *"Gentleman"*, was allotted only about an acre and a half.

Thomas Hopcraft, Churchwarden, but evidently not classed as a gentleman, received 55 acres and 13 perches in settlement upon his wife, Elizabeth and a further 17 acres 2 roods and 9 perches from the will of his father, William, who must have died quite recently. He increased his holdings by buying the rights to 7 acres or so from James Blackwell, who lived in Brackley and had land in Hinton-in-the-Hedges and three smaller plots from John Toppin and Jonas Phillips, both of whom are described as owning cottages in Evenley. His allotments were on the Heath, on either side of the Buckingham road. He had already succeeded his father as tenant of land in Astwick belonging to Magdalen College and forming part of the Evenley Rectory land. This lay on the other side of the Oxford Road, adjoining his new land and forming a substantial holding. It is interesting to see that in a future generation, Barnett John Hopcraft of Evenley was Commissioner for the Brackley enclosure of 1829, while a later Robert Weston was one of his clerks.

The other individual mentioned in both the Act and the preamble to the Award, is Joseph Painter, who is shown on the map as having property on the Village Green. He was allotted 88 acres 2 roods and 11 perches to the west of the village, between Hinton and Astwick.

There were a total of 32 individuals allotted land, including those who sold their allotments. Most of the allotments were quite small, apart from 81 acres to the Rev. William Bowles (as lessee of Magdalen College) in trust for his two youngest sisters. One, that of Thomas Smith, is only 11 perches. As for the other allotments specified in the Act, the Vicar, Churchwardens and Overseers of the Poor received 22 acres 2 roods and 2 perches on the Heath to compensate for the loss of the furze by the poor. This was next to two other smaller allotments, one for the Churchwardens and one other for the Vicar, Churchwardens and Overseers of the Poor in trust for the poor widows of the parish. The two allotments for stone pits were 1 acre 1 rood and 28 perches on Bicester Hill, which is now Evenley Common and 2 roods at the end of Broad Lane, which just about corresponds to the triangle of land cut off by the new course of Broad Lane where it now meets the A43.

How many of the landowners lived in Evenley? Of the larger proprietors, probably only Sir Francis Basset, who still spent some time on the family estate in Cornwall, Thomas Hopcraft and possibly Joseph Painter were resident. It is unlikely that John Finden, the Vicar, spent much time in the village. He certainly employed a curate. In 1779, this was John Pyefinch.

Of the remaining proprietors, William Strange was a small farmer in Turweston, James Blackwell kept the *"Swan"* in Brackley and John Butterfield came from a prominent Brackley family, while William Thomas Bowles was the son of Rev. Thomas Bowles, a previous Vicar of Brackley. One of his sisters was married to a Somerset vicar and the other to a *"gentleman"*, but is unlikely to have lived in Evenley. Their father was a scholar who had married into the Lisle family, the previous Lords of the Manor and he was later the central figure in a notorious religious scandal in Wales. George Thomas was acting as clerk to the Commissioners and had a house and a business as an attorney in Brackley High St. His son, also George, is a witness to several of the signatures at the end of the Award. Robert Weston lived at Aynho, while John Wills appears in the 1777 Militia List for Newbottle.

Definitely resident in Evenley were the two Thomas Souths and John South, who all appear in the Militia Lists, John Holton, a cordwainer, John Smith, the miller, Thomas Smith, a maltster who owned the Old Manor House and William Holton. William was a prominent villager, a butcher who was a Churchwarden and Village Constable in 1777, when he drew up the Evenley Militia List.

All the roads, bridleways, footpaths and private roads, that were to run across the enclosed lands, were specified in the Award and most of these still exist. Three roads were to be sixty feet wide, Oxford Road, the Buckingham Road and the road around the Green. Other public roads, including some which have now shrunk to footpaths, were to be at least forty feet wide, while bridleways had to be ten feet wide. A width of twenty feet is specified for the five private roads described in the Award. Some of the names are interesting; what is now School Lane is described as Kennish Lane, while the footpath from Church Lane to Brackley is described as the Horse Lane.

At the end of the document there is a table dealing with the expenses of the fencing, the Commissioners' fees and the general expenses, showing what each of the proprietors had to pay as their share. The first two columns of this table are headed *"Inequality of Fencing"* and provided a means of sharing out the costs of fencing and ditching more fairly between the proprietors. Those who were fortunate enough to have been given plots lying next to old enclosures, or which already had good boundary fences or hedges, would obviously not have incurred as much expense as those receiving plots in completely open expanses of land, so the Commissioners devised a scheme whereby some proprietors paid money into a fund, which was then distributed to those with a more than proportionately fair share of the fencing. For instance, Sir Francis Basset must have benefited considerably from pre-existing fences, for he paid out £69.16s.1¾d, whilst John Stevens received £12.4s.6d towards the cost of his work.

The Commissioners were paid a total of £151.12s.0¼d and the general expenses came to £1,621.13s.9½d. The expenses were divided up proportionately between the proprietors, with by far the lion's share falling to Sir Francis Basset. He paid £42.17s.8½d to the Commissioners and £493.0s.9½d in general expenses, on top of the inequality of fencing payment. The smallest expense was incurred by the Feoffees of the Poor of Brackley, who received an allotment of 2 roods 18 perches and whose total expenses came to 19s.4¾d.

As has been noted, the completed Award was signed by the Commissioners at a public meeting at the *"Crown"* in Brackley on March 23rd 1780. The signatures of Francis Basset, John Finden, John Burrows, George Thomas, Mary Davis, the Steward of Magdalen College, John Stevens and Thomas Hopcraft, with the mark of Ann Davis, were also added. The new proprietors had to fence their allotments with *"posts and double rails with back ditches and banks up to the lower rails on or before the 5th of April next"*, although gaps were to be left until 1st May for the convenient removal of *"trees, underwood, thorns, hedges, bushes, furze or shrubs growing"*. Permanent hedges or walls were to be put in place by 25th December. Instead of the largely undifferentiated open fields and large tract of furze-covered heath of the past, a landscape of smaller hedged, or walled fields and straightened, metalled roads came into being. This was essentially the landscape that we see around the village today.

Part of the 1779 Enclosure Map

Views of Evenley circa 1900 - 1930

**View across the Green toward the south side,
showing the road that once existed**

Cutting the Grass on the Green

45

The Manor House in Church Lane

View across the Green toward Dormer Row and the north side

View of cottages on the north side

46

THE 1867 EVENLEY STRIKE

March 1867 was an eventful month in the Brackley and Buckingham areas. A series of strikes occurred among agricultural labourers in the district, who were protesting against their low wages and the impoverished lives they led.

It is certainly true that farm workers were wretchedly paid. It has been estimated that at the time, the average working wage was thirty-one shillings a week, while farm labourers in this area were usually paid ten or eleven shillings. Out of this, they had to find one or two shillings for rent and food prices were rising. Although trades unions had existed for some twenty years, there was at this time no union for agricultural workers; that would come five years later, in 1872. There were some organised attempts to improve the farm labourer's lot, but these mainly consisted of committees set up to help emigration to other parts of England, where farm wages were higher, usually in the north. There was one such in Buckingham and a poster advertising the scheme was displayed in the grocer's shop of Thomas Judge in Bridge Street, Brackley.

Thomas Judge was a well-known local Radical and Nonconformist, a thorn in the side of the largely Conservative and Anglican establishment. He was a campaigner for Parliamentary reform and an advocate of better wages and conditions for the local farm workers. In December 1866, he had organised a Reform Meeting in Brackley attended by between two and three thousand people, where speakers had called for universal male suffrage and other reforms, including better agricultural wages. Two brass bands played and Chinese lanterns and torches created a festival atmosphere. The reporter from the Banbury Guardian found it all so enthralling that he nearly missed the last train home! Unfortunately, some of the participants lingered too long in the *"Locomotive"* afterwards, some fighting broke out and the police had to be called. This allowed the Chairman of the local magistrates, the Rev. Francis Litchfield of Farthinghoe, to roundly condemn those who organised political meetings, adding that the defendants should be punished for their folly, in going to such a meeting at all.

Articles and letters in the local press at the time make quite clear the opposition from local establishment figures to reformist ideas, but the reformers were also keen letter writers. A letter signed *"A Farm Labourer"* printed in the Bicester Herald of March 9th, shows the clear link between the movement for Parliamentary reform and demands for better wages. The writer describes how *"the agricultural labourers round here have been having only 9s. and 10s. per week during this winter, with bread at 8d. per 1/2lb. loaf. We have had several Reform Meetings round here, at Brackley and Buckingham. After these meetings, the labourers in some instances obtained 1s. per week more and in some cases 2s., without any difficulty. Some of us workingmen in this village thought we ought to have 2s. per day and 1s. for Sunday work. Because we made this application we had part of our week's wages put into our hands and were dismissed there and then that night...This feeling towards us is partly owing to our seeking a vote in the country that thinks it is fair to tax our 10s. per week"*. The village was Gawcott.

At the beginning of March, farm workers in Croughton came out on strike and seemed to have obtained a rise of one shilling a week without much difficulty. Encouraged, some thirty men came out on strike in Evenley a week later, about the same time as twenty-eight farm labourers struck in Gawcott. The Gawcott strike was the longer lasting and it gained wide publicity. It was Reported in the Daily Telegraph, in a rather mocking piece that contained the line, *"Where in the world should we look for peace, perfection and bucolic bliss, when even the sacred soil of Bucks, is not free from the spirit of change?"*, although they did seem to agree that farm wages were rather low. An article in

The Times, however, led to donations from other parts of the country to the strike fund, including the sum of £3 from "a Landowner and Clergyman". After a week or two, the strikers achieved their rise. The successful strike eventually came to the notice of Karl Marx, who referred to it in a footnote in *'Das Kapital'*.

The Evenley strike was not to be so successful. Not all of the workers came out and on three occasions men who were still at work were harassed and attacked by strikers, leading to prosecutions for assault at a Special Petty Sessions at Brackley on Saturday, March 16th. The proceedings were very fully reported in the Banbury Guardian of March 21st. In the first case, seven of the strikers, William Walton, Daniel Young, George Sheppard, William Davis, Thomas Mander, Alfred Jordan and Thomas Stowe, were charged with assaulting Thomas Golding. He was on his way to work for Mr Railton, who farmed the Rectory Farm land. Various witnesses appeared for both the prosecution and the defence, but their accounts conflict somewhat.

The incident took place on Tuesday, March 12th, at about 7.00 in the morning near the school, when Thomas Golding, who did not know about the strike, was accosted by the defendants and others. A scuffle certainly took place and it seems as if a crowd quickly gathered. One of the witnesses speaks of as many as fifty people being present. Golding claimed to have been struck by George Sheppard and to have defended himself with the fork he was carrying. This turned into a general tussle for the fork, during which Golding was, in his words, "pretty much mauled and pulled about". However, some witnesses said that Golding struck the first blow.

In the second case, William Heeley a blacksmith, was said to have been attacked on Monday, March 11th, by Thomas and Edward Stowe, William Holton and Joseph Sheppard, while on his way with James Jones to feed Mr Railton's sheep. Quite a large crowd of men and boys seem to have thrown stones at and threatened the two men, but Heeley recognised only the four who were charged. The next day, similar threats and stone-throwing occurred, when the two men were again going to feed the sheep and John Abbott was charged with threatening James Jones with a stick *"almost as big as a besom stick"*, although his defence lawyer claimed it was *"only a small nutstick"*.

Thomas Judge, the radical Brackley grocer, was called as a character witness by the defence and affirmed that he knew all the defendants, had had conversations and dealings with them and had the highest opinion of them as honest,

Thomas Judge's Shop in Brackley

upright, straightforward men. He also believed them to be sober men, who had never before been brought before the Magistrates for any reason.

Unfortunately, Judge and the Chairman of the Bench, the Rev. Francis Litchfield were old adversaries and Litchfield took the opportunity to berate Judge for encouraging the men to strike. He also said that it was Judge's fault that they found themselves in their present predicament, even suggesting that he had done it so that they might have more money to spend in his shop. When Judge asked if he might speak in reply, Litchfield refused him, saying that this was not a place for *'speechifying'*. All the men were found guilty apart from William Davis, Thomas Mander and Alfred Jordan, as it was clear from the witnesses' statements that they had not been among the attackers. The fines ranged from 2s.6d. to £2, with costs. Thomas Judge, whose cousin was married to one of the men, paid some of the fines and others paid their own, but some of the strikers had to borrow the money from their employers, to be repaid at a later date, presumably out of their wages. Most of the men returned to work the following Monday at their old wage.

In 1872, the Agricultural Workers' Union was founded at Wellesbourne in Warwickshire and the movement quickly spread. A meeting to form a branch in Brackley took place in June of that year, with Thomas Judge as Chairman. By the end of the year, the Banbury Union, which included Brackley and Evenley, had 2,290 members. The acquitted William Davis became secretary of the Evenley Branch of the National Agricultural Labourers' Union and was an active trade unionist for almost twenty years.

"The wages at this time were two and six weekly for boys starting work from school, and that is the wage I received when I left school (circa 1912). A daymen's wages were twelve shillings weekly, and the horsemen (carters and stockmen) thirteen shillings weekly, with a shilling a week extra for Sunday work to attend their animals, horses, cattle and sheep on Sundays. This wage was general around and adjoining counties. There were many families brought up on twelve to thirteen shillings weekly, and with three, four, five or six children kept in clothes and fed in those days and going to school happy and clean."

Life was Like That – 1976 – W. Buggins

EVENLEY HALL

Evenley Hall was built by Francis Bassett (1715-1769), shortly after his purchase of the estate from the beneficiaries of the Will of one William Price, circa 1735.

The mid 18th Century Hall was probably erected on the site of an earlier building, but records of that time are not clear on this point.

Evenley Hall

Historians of the Bassett Family have established that Francis Bassett *"lived in Oxfordshire or Thereabouts"* and in 1756, he inherited the Bassett estates in Cornwall and Devon.

It is not known why the young man was residing away from his native South West, but knowledge of his family background and likely social standing (his inheritance included 26 manors), may help to explain his reasons for building a mansion of Evenley Hall's scale and grandeur. The earliest known record of the form of the first Evenley Hall is a map of the parish, made in about 1780 A.D. At this time, the property exchanged hands twice, being sold in 1786 by Francis Bassett's son (also named Francis) to George Rush and four years later, by Rush to Herbert Gwynne Browne.

In 1803, Gwynne Browne's daughter Georgina became the owner. She was first married to Pryce Edwards and then remarried in 1810 to the Hon. Philip Sydney Pierrepont, 5th son of Charles, the first Earl of Manvers, from Thoresby Hall in Nottinghamshire. A memorial window to Georgina and the next owner of the Hall, Colonel Campbell, can be seen in the church.

The last family to be resident was the Allen family. William Henry Allen and his wife Ellen Moulson took up residence in 1890, but had the difficult task of rebuilding the Hall after a disastrous fire. An excellent job was done by the builders and folk in Brackley still remember their grandparents being involved. A note about the fire in 1897 recalls that it took place after Christmas time and the temperature was so low that the water froze.

The Banbury Guardian gave a full account of this disaster in its edition dated Jan 28th 1897.

According to Capt. Norris, the fire tender from Steane Park was sent, but to no avail and the building was severely damaged. William Allen's niece remembers being called by her nurse to the window of Brackley House where she lived, in order to see Evenley Hall on fire. She recalled that she was just 2 years old at the time.

Things quietened down after that and the country life of squire and village settled down to the well-ordered system of those days. William Henry and his son Major Allen who followed him, were remembered by the village for the water supply, electricity and the cricket team. The Allen's had their own cricket pitch at the top of the parkland. The end of the era was in sight however and in 1936, the Major died and was buried in Evenley Churchyard. It was then decided that the whole estate, a few farms, fields and houses together with Evenley Hall and the parkland, should be sold off at auction

The sale took place in 1938 and many villagers took the opportunity of purchasing their own property. It was at this point in time that a businessman Frederick Newman Kidd from Dartford in Kent, who owned a brewery, was looking for a country retreat, particularly as the shadow of war was looming. Evenley Hall fitted his requirements, so he and his family moved there just before the outbreak of World War II. His daughter, Bobbie, who was about 12 years old then, returned to visit the Hall in 1997 and spoke about that time. She said that they had only been there for about six months when the army arrived asking them to leave at the end of the week. They left and went to Bournemouth never to return and the East Yorks Yeomanry took their place. The army added some extra buildings and along the drive built hard standing plots for the parking of army vehicles. The army stayed until D-Day in June 1944 and were then followed for a brief period by groups of evacuees from London, where the flying bombs were causing much concern.

In 1941, Mr Kidd heard Lord Stamp give an appeal on the radio, on behalf of the National Children's Home, for property or other gifts to help expand their work of child-care in the country. The National Children's Home (now called NCH Action for Children)

was a Methodist Children's Charity, founded by the Rev. Thomas Bowman Stephenson, a Methodist Minister, in 1869. Frederick Kidd responded to this appeal most generously by offering Evenley Hall and Parkland to the NCH and this offer was gladly accepted and very much appreciated. A sad story concerning the appeal was that only 5 days after making the appeal, Lord Stamp was killed by enemy action in London.

It was therefore in 1947 that a new phase in the story of Evenley hall commenced. Mr William T. Clark came up from South Wales to set up a home for children and very soon the Hall and its grounds echoed to the sounds of children enjoying the delights of a place where space was free for all kinds of activity.

Mr Clark, known as Bill to his friends, soon had established the care programme for these children, who through no fault of their own, had to live away from their families. The caring was in the form of family groups, where up to 12 children, boys and girls, lived together, cared for by a Sister of the NCH. The sisters, who were specially trained at the NCH training college in London, were dedicated workers who gave their lives to the care of the children.

When one new youngster asked one of the Sisters while she was putting him to bed, *"who will get me up"*, she replied, *"I puts thee to bed and I gets thee up"*.

Sadness was never far away when one considers that most of the children would have given anything to be in a normal loving family home of their own. Even so, there was the knowledge that if this could not be, then Evenley Hall was an excellent second place. Children who had been deprived of their homes found real freedom in the grounds. There were lawns to play on, woods to keep as nature reserves and trees to climb.

When the end of schooling was reached and sometimes before, plans would have been worked on, in order that the children could return to their home area and find suitable openings for employment or further education. This was quite a difficult move, even though most of the young people were eagerly looking forward to it.

In the early 1980's, the social services decided to stop sending children to places such as Evenley Hall and instead, asked the NCH to consider offering a residential and day service, for young people with learning disabilities.

In 1984, seven young students arrived to take up a place at the Evenley Hall Community Project and participate in a *"Training for Life"* programme. Numbers continually increased and the training programmes steadily evolved. By 1997, many of the students were able to carry out some form of *"out-work"* and attend evening classes in Brackley and day courses at Banbury College.

The supporters of the work, the Friends of Evenley Hall, were a tremendous asset over the years. Some volunteers came regularly each week to provide essential extra hands to share the skill making tasks and all of them found it to be a rewarding time.

It was however apparent to the executive committee of NCH Action for Children that this aspect of their organisation might not be covered by charitable status. It therefore became necessary for them to enter into discussion with the Social services, to look for another charity to take over the work.

After about 2 years of planning and discussion, the Shaftesbury Society was chosen from a short list of organisations to manage the project, which commenced in January 1997.

The Hall and its Parkland still belonged to NCH Action for Children and the plan was for the property to be sold and the income put back into childcare. Meanwhile the Shaftesbury Society was given a 5-year lease of the Hall to continue the work and plan for their future.

This ultimately resulted in changes at the Hall in June 2001 when all the resident students transferred into homes in Brackley in order to live within the community and be able to take part in local activities more easily.

The Hall was sold and by September 2001 it was once more in the hands of a private family.

"The parkland around the Hall was well wooded and carried a large number of oak, elm, beech and chestnut trees, and many had their branches tied with strong iron bands and chains. Today there are none of these trees standing on the eastern and southern faces of Evenley Hall. The Front Park remains today as it was in the years 1900 to 1914. The Mill Farm was added to the estate in 1912"

"The park and pasture lands on the eastern and southern sides of Evenley Hall, having been detached as part of that estate, were separated from the Front Park and Evenley Hall in 1939. These acres carried a large number of fine old ash and elm trees that had been protected and kept together with massive iron chains."

Life was Like That – 1976 – W. Buggins

EVENLEY HALL ESTATE SALE 1938

NORTHAMPTONSHIRE

On the borders of Oxfordshire and Buckinghamshire. Adjoining the Ancient Market Town and Borough of Brackley. On the L.N.E. and L.M.S. Railways. One hour and ten minutes by Express Train to London. 21 miles Northampton. 20 miles Oxford. 60 miles London (by road). 7 miles Buckingham. 9 miles Banbury. 10 miles Bicester. Hunting : Bicester and Grafton Packs.

Illustrated Particulars, Plans and Conditions of Sale

of

THE FREEHOLD RESIDENTIAL, AGRICULTURAL AND SPORTING ESTATE

known as

Evenley Hall Estate

comprising

THE CHARMING XVIIIth CENTURY MANSION

distinguished as

Evenley Hall

of moderate size and delightful design, about 400 feet above sea level, commanding extensive views, and standing within gardens of great maturity and magnificence. Four Reception Rooms. Billiards Room. Twenty-three Principal, Secondary and Staff Bedrooms. Four Bathrooms. Ample Domestic Offices. Stabling and Garage. Outhouses. Walled Kitchen Garden and Glasshouses

The Superb Pleasure Gardens

include Three Tennis Courts, Rose and Water Gardens, Yew Hedges and Topiary.

Well-timbered Grounds and Park

Main Electricity   Excellent Water Supply   Good Drainage System

also

THREE FIRST-CLASS FARMS

all equipped with Good Houses and ample Farm Buildings, comprising :—

The Dairy Holding, known as ROAD FARM, 94 ACRES
(with vacant possession)

The Mixed Farm, known as MIDDLE FARM, 127 ACRES
(with vacant possession)

and

The Mixed Holding, known as EVENLEY HALL FARM, 233 ACRES
(let on yearly, Lady Day, Tenancy)

THE OLD-WORLD VILLAGE OF EVENLEY

including 54 Cottages. The Village Green, Schoolhouse, School. Two Houses and Gardens, Six Allotment Enclosures. Valuable Timbered Woodlands and Plantations. Small Holdings. Twelve Choice Enclosures of Accommodation Pasture Land and Seven Fertile Arable Fields, some having long frontage to the Oxford main and other roads, and suitable for Building development. Seven Enclosures of Meadow Land.   The Evenley Village Water Supply.

The whole Estate contains an area of about

1,080 ACRES

(ALL TITHE FREE)

which

FOX & SONS

are favoured with instructions to SELL BY AUCTION, in 94 Lots,

AT THE TOWN HALL, BRACKLEY

on Tuesday July 26th, 1938

in Two Sessions at 10.30 a.m. and 2.30 p.m. precisely (unless previously sold privately)

Vacant Possession of the Residence, Gardens, Parkland and Woodlands, Road Farm and Middle Farm, numerous Small Holdings, some Cottages and Land in hand, will be given on completion of the purchase.

Solicitors : MESSRS. LACEY & SON, 17, Avenue Road, Bournemouth.
Land Agent : MR. H. P. STACE, Brackley, Northamptonshire.
Auctioneers : MESSRS. FOX & SONS, Bournemouth and Southampton.
Telegrams : Homefinder, Bournemouth   *Telephone :* Bournemouth 2386 (4 lines)

RICHMOND HILL PRINTING WORKS, LTD., BOURNEMOUTH

In July 1938, the Evenley Hall estate, encompassing some 1,080 acres, was sold by public auction. The Hall with its 3 farms, together with the village of Evenley and its water supply, were all sold. Extracts from the sale catalogue follow, together with photographs of some of the houses in the village that were part of the sale.

Evenley Village and Green

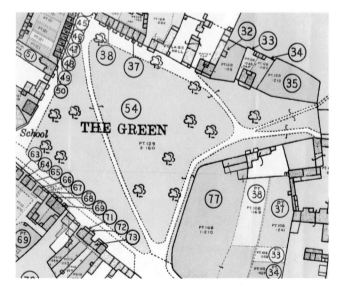

(Coloured *Mauve* on Sale Plan No. 2)

THE VERY ATTRACTIVE DETACHED

Schoolhouse with Garden

Extending to an area of about

19 perches

Situate in Evenley Village, and being Ordnance No. Pt. 121 (.120 acres).

The House is substantially built of stone and slate, and contains :—

ON THE GROUND FLOOR—

ENTRANCE HALL, with tiled floor. DINING ROOM, about 13ft. square, fitted with tiled firegrate and recessed open shelves. SITTING ROOM, 13ft. 9ins. by 12ft. 6ins., with combustion grate and two recessed cupboards. KITCHEN, with portable stove, copper, earthenware sink (hot and cold water), dresser. Soft Water Pump to outside tank of about 2,000 gallons. (The Electric Heater and connections are claimed to be the property of the occupier.) PANTRY, with fitted range of three cupboards.

ON THE FIRST FLOOR—

SPACIOUS LANDING. Two large BEDROOMS, each with fitted firegrate and recessed cupboard. BATHROOM, with fitted bath.

ON THE SECOND FLOOR—

Two large BEDROOMS.

Main electric light and Evenley Village water laid on.

Outside : Stone and galvanised Coal House and Pail Closet. Walled Garden.

Let, with other property, to Northampton-shire County Council, on lease expiring September 29th, 1963, at an apportioned rental of £15 per annum. Tenants pay rates.

Land Tax as assessed.

This Lot is sold subject to a right of way over part of the South boundary adjoining the School Building on Lot 53 for access to the Store Room and Coal Cellar (belonging to Lot 53), in favour of the Purchaser of Lot 53.

See footnote to Lot 55 as to right of way granted by lease dated 8th October, 1921.

See General Remarks and Stipulations as to " Water Supplies."

Lot 52 –The School House

Lot 58 – A Cottage

61

LOT 58
(Coloured *Yellow* on Sale Plan No. 1)

A VERY ATTRACTIVE
OLD-WORLD DETACHED

Cottage
with Garden

Extending to an area of about
22 perches

Situate at Evenley, and being Ordnance
No. 236 (.139 acres).

The Cottage is built of stone with tiled
roof, and contains : Open Porch. Sitting
Room, with firegrate. Kitchen, with
fitted oven stove and three cupboards.
Scullery, with earthenware sink (cold
water tap). Larder. Back Kitchen.
Two Bedrooms (one having fireplace).

Outside : Pail Closet.

Water is laid on from the Evenley Village
supply.

Occupied by Mr. T. Peverell (formerly an
Estate employee). Landlord pays rates.

Land Tax as assessed.

Lot 25 A Cottage

Lots 38 and 37

Lot 56 –A Cottage

Lots 32, 33 and 34

62

Lot 31 – Evenley Hall Farm

Lots 76 and 75

Lots 50 to 41

Lot 53 – The School

Lots 67 to 62

Lots 69 and 68

Lots 74 to 71

Village ladies circa 1910

63

(Reservoir, Pump House and Well—Coloured *Pink* on Sale Plans Nos. 1 and 2)

THE
EVENLEY WATER SUPPLY

Within Enclosure Ordnance No. 146, adjoining Evenley Village on the West, is a Well of a depth of about 50 feet. In the Well are two pumps. Above is a Wind Pump, and adjoining is a brick and galvanised iron Pump or Engine House containing an electric dynamo, on main electricity supply, with pulleys and shafting connected to the pump, for auxiliary purposes. The water is conveyed by pipes to a Reservoir of a capacity of about 20,000 gallons, situate within the same enclosure. Therefrom, water is piped in a South-westerly direction under the same enclosure, and thence under Enclosure Ordnance No. 120 (Lot 55) and then proceeds under the garden of Lot 50 to the Village, and supplying the following Estate properties :—

Lots 41 to 50 (one tap in garden of Lot 47).
Lots 36, 37 and 38 (one tap at the back of Cottage No. 50 on Lot 37).
Lots 39 and 40 (one tap in the garden of Lot 39).
Lot 32 (laid on to backyard).
Lots 33 and 34 (one tap in garden of Lot 33).
Lot 31 (laid on to Evenley Hall Farmhouse and Yards).
Lots 51, 52 and 53 (laid on separately).
Lots 62 to 69 (one tap at the back of Cottage on Lot 66).
Lot 70 (laid on to Cottage).
Lots 71 to 74 (one tap at the back of the Cottage on Lot 72).
Lots 75, 76 and 78 (one tap on Lot 76).

A water supply is also piped Northwards to the following Estate properties :—

Lot 56 (laid on to Cottage).
Lot 57 (the Farm Buildings).
Lot 58 (laid on to the Cottage).
Lot 25 (Middle Farm House, Cottage, Laundry and Farm Buildings).
Lot 1 (Road, Farmhouse, Farm Buildings and Yard).

Water is also laid on to other properties which do not belong to the Vendors, viz :—

						Rent per annum.		
No.						£	s.	d.
1.	Messrs. Hopcraft and Norris, Ltd.	...	...	...	...	2	0	0
2.	Rev. G. A. Ward-Jackson ...	...	...	...	...		5	0
3.	Mr. Chas. Holton ...	...	...	...	...	1	0	0
4.	Mr. E. J. Law ...	...	...	...	...		10	0
5.	Mr. D. J. Martin ...	...	...	...	...	1	0	0
6.	Mr. T. H. Turvey	...	...	...	...	1	0	0
7.	Mrs. E. W. Tetley	...	...	...	...		5	0	0

As regards No. 1, *see* footnote hereto.   £10 15 0

There are agreements relating to the above Nos., 2 to 7, inclusive.

Area of Reservoir, Pump House and Well, Ord. No. Pt. 146, .055 acres (9 perches).

One shilling per annum is payable for pipes laid across property on the North side of Evenley Village.

The Purchaser of this Lot shall have all necessary rights of entry on the Lots mentioned in the above particulars of this Lot, and on any other Lots through, across or under which any pipes and connections forming part of the water system are laid, for the purpose of inspection, repair, renewal and maintenance of the water system, such Lots being sold subject thereto.

This Lot is sold subject to :—

(1) A right for the Vendors to receive free of charge a supply of water as at present enjoyed in respect of any Lots remaining unsold.

(2) A right for Messrs. Hopcraft and Norris, Ltd., or other the owners or occupiers for the time being of the " Red Lion " Inn, Evenley, to a supply of such water as may from time to time be available on payment of a yearly charge of £2 per annum and if any additional supply is required a right to take such additional supply if available subject to such additional annual charge as may be mutually agreed.

EXTRACTS FROM A LETTER WRITTEN BY MRS. CICELY SPENCER TO HER GRANDSON

Mrs Spencer bought the old Manor in 1939 and lived in the village for sixty years. In 1993 she wrote a letter to her grandson in which she talks about life in Evenley in the 1930's.

"The village was just coming to the end of the way things had been with a Squire at Evenley Hall who owned all the cottages and employed many of the men to work on the land, or in the garden and stables. Other local men worked on the railway, riding their bicycles to work. In the evenings, they cultivated their allotments and the vegetables they grew were "half their keep", as one man told me. There were large families, as often the girl married the man next door, or at least someone in the village, making big family connections. The children went to the village school and home to their mothers for their dinners. On Sundays, the men and boys who could sing were in surplices in the church choir. Old customs were still observed and on 1st May, the school children went round the village carrying garlands of flowers and singing songs. There was always a bonfire on the Village Green on 5th November.

There was no sanitation in the cottages and only an earth closet at the bottom of the garden. When it had to be emptied the allotments came in useful and they certainly produced excellent vegetables! The wells were still in use in the early 1930's, although the Squire had put in standpipes for some of the cottages. There was a supply of water pumped by a windmill from where the Manor had its water. It was then pumped by hand to a storage tank in the attic.

There was a small shop and carrier (a man with a horse and cart who would shop for the villagers twice a week) and a muffin man who came round with a basket on his head, ringing his bell and selling crumpets and muffins. When there was a funeral, the coffin was taken to church on a bier, a long, flat carriage on wheels, which was pulled by hand, with the family walking behind.

There were houses on three sides of the Green, one little row of cottages, Dormer Row, built by an old lady who lived at Evenley Hall. She didn't want people gossiping outside their houses as she drove by, so they were built without front doors! There were magnificent elms on the Green and a road went across from the Old Manor corner to the pub. Sadly, the elms were killed by Dutch elm disease. A farmer walked across the Green from the farm to his house carrying pails of milk on a yoke across his shoulders.

Some time after the war, new houses were built in the village and the village changed. Cars began to appear round the Green as there were no garages and the new word 'commuter' came into being. Cottages that were sold by the Evenley Hall estate for £100 were fetching thousands of pounds. I remember when the row of houses up Bone Hill (School Lane) used the bank opposite their cottages for making fires and boiling their clothes and cooking on them. I don't know why they chose to do this, as there was a common boiler in 'a hovel' for the use of the cottagers and a deep well for their water."

Mrs. Spencer died in 1999 and her name is commemorated in a small close of houses which were built on the allotment site which she had owned, opposite the Manor House.

A WALK AROUND THE VILLAGE

William Buggins in his book on Evenley, *'Life Was Like That'*, states that *"Few records seem to exist, to show what Evenley looked like before 1865, except for what was handed down by mouth from one generation to another by men, who could neither read nor write"*.

It appears that Evenley consisted of many thatched cottages, which served the farms of the time and that most of them became dangerous and unfit to live in.

There was a line of cottages from near the Church to the Manor House, continuing toward Lower Farm, now Evenley Farm. There was another line running from the school corner, down to the Manor House, like an inverted letter 'L'. There were no houses on the eastern side of the village and only two or three on the southern side. It is said, that it was Mr. Sydney Pierrepont who planned the village as it is today, circa 1850-60.

Most of the thatched cottages were pulled down during the Pierrepont's time at Evenley and many of them were rebuilt and the Green laid out as it is today, with a road across the Green from the Manor House to the Red Lion to give an easy way out of the village for horse drawn vehicles. This road was later closed by the County Council and grassed over, making a huge improvement to the Green for the purposes of football, cricket and the provision of a larger area for children to play, in safety from motor and other traffic.

The school was also a thatched building in the early 1800s. The new one built in its place bears the date 1834.

THE GREEN

The original conservation area of Evenley was designated in 1966 and covers the central part of the village around a very large open Green of approximately 2½ acres with a cricket pitch in the centre. It is lined on three sides by mainly 18th- and 19th-century houses and cottages in squared uncoursed limestone, or limestone rubble with Welsh slate, or clay tile roofs, many of which have distinctive bands of alternating red and black tiles. No. 23 has what are described as fish scale tiles. Most of these properties are Grade II listed. On the fourth side of the green, there are modern detached brick houses, which are softened by mature front gardens and a number of adjoining trees. There is one 19th-century cottage.

Cricket on the Green

In 1987, the conservation area was extended to include the long cul-de-sac of Church Lane which extends from the north corner of the Green to the parish church of St George. It is thought that the area around the Green developed at a later stage than the medieval village, which clustered around the church, at the western end of Church Lane.

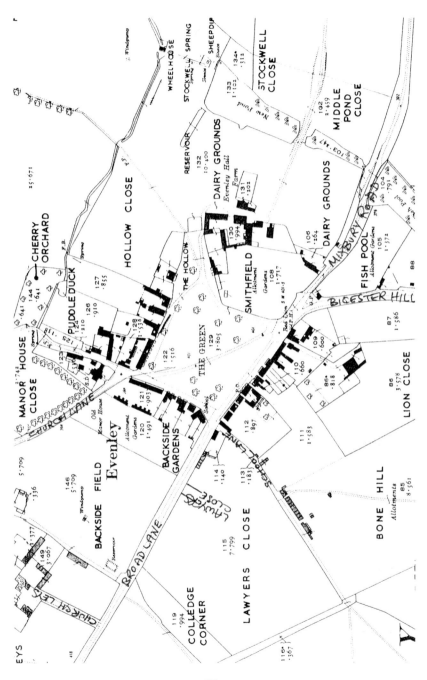

69

The oldest complete building remaining on the Green is 17th Century so it is assumed, that it was during the 17th and 18th Centuries that the Green began to be developed. However, there are several cottages dating from the 1860's and 70's that were built as part of a planned development around the Green by the Pierrepont family, who lived in Evenley Hall at that time. During this period, a number of 18th-century houses were also remodelled to create a more coherent appearance, including the Red Lion public house in the southeast corner. There are four pairs of semi-detached cottages with side entrances, three on the south side and one, standing alone, at the east end of the north side. These were built as part of the Pierrepont family redevelopment, as well as two terraces of eight cottages, Nos. 5-12 (Dormer Row) on the west side and eight to the north, Nos. 14-21. There is no number 13!

Although there have been minor detailed alterations to some of these buildings in recent years, the estate influence and the consistent use of limestone has created a particularly harmonious character around the Green. Large gabled dormer windows breaking through the eaves line are another distinctive feature of several houses, as are the Victorian chimney pots, which are made of stone, unlike the older brick ones.

West side of the Green

WEST SIDE

At the south end of the west side stands the Village Hall, which was built by Mrs Pierrepont and the vicar, John Butler Harrison, for use as a Day and Sunday School in 1834. The elevation facing the Green has two sets of striking triple-arched timber windows and a prominent stone chimneystack at each gable end.

Next to the Village Hall stands No.2 The Green, which used to be the School House and was part of the planned development of the Green. There is a date stone over the front door: 1869. No.3 is an 18th-century building. The date on the front is 1790 but the house is thought to date from an earlier period. The remains of bakery ovens were found when the house was reconstructed and it may at one time have been the village bakery. It is the only house along the West Side without dormer windows and it used to be thatched before the third storey was added. The stable at the back is now the kitchen.

No.4 used to be two houses. The south side, with only two storeys, was a cottage, which is now incorporated into the attached next-door three-storey house. The cottage was divided into two 2-up 2-down cottages, with a second door on the south side, traces of which can be seen in the wall where it was 'stoned up'. There is a window there now and the wooden lintel above clearly belongs to a door, as it is much wider than the window. An addition at the side used to be a Smithy.

Nos.5-12 is a row of terraced cottages built by the Pierreponts of Evenley Hall. Between Nos. 4 and 5, there is an alleyway, that leads to the back gardens where the front doors were originally, with letter boxes where the postman still delivers the mail. Apparently, Mrs Pierrepont did not wish to see the tenants 'gossiping' at their front doors, thus lowering the tone of the Green! Doors on the Green were added between, it is thought, the late 1960's and 1980's. However, <u>nos.11 and 12</u> still do not have one.

NORTH SIDE

No. 23 & The Shop & Post Office

The second row of terraced houses built by the Pierreponts were <u>Nos.14 – 21</u>. The last four are now owned by South Northants Council. <u>No.22</u> used to be two cottages, one of which housed a family with five children. <u>No. 23</u> is the present village shop, with a Victorian post box, dated 1873, set into the wall. The deeds of the building indicate that part of the original fabric dates back to 1530. No 23 has been in its time, a wheelwright's workshop, a malt-house barn and in 1925, Major Allen converted it into a social club for the benefit of the village.

Subsequently, it became a shop, which eventually closed in 1989. In 1991, the premises reopened as a shop and post office and today it thrives as an important part of village life.

<u>No.24</u> is conspicuous for being the only thatched house remaining around the Green, with its gable end 'to the road'. It dates back to the 17th century and is, therefore, the oldest house remaining on the Green

24 The Green

24/25 The Green

Back from the road and unseen from it is a cottage, <u>No.26</u>, which stands behind <u>No.25</u> that faces the Green. According to a local resident, a barn or large room at the back was used for the laying-out of the dead. <u>Nos.28 & 29</u> are a pair of semi-detached cottages standing alone on the other side of the lane leading to <u>No.26</u>. <u>No.28</u> has one wood lintel and one stone lintel over the front windows and two stone lintels at the side. The lintels above the windows of <u>No.29</u> are all wood. There appears to be no <u>No. 27</u>.

35 The Green – in shade

The village stocks stood at the North-east of the village, near to an elm tree known as the 'Stocks Tree'. these were taken down and burned when the Green was laid out, circa 1850. There were nine elm trees on the Green from 1905 – 1917. The 'Stock Tree' had the top blown off and was a hollow stump, i.e. during the early 1900's. There were four trees left in 1976. Later, due to Elm Disease, they were all removed.

EAST SIDE

The east side consists mainly of modern detached brick houses but includes one 19th-century cottage, <u>No.35</u>. According to the deeds, it used to be an off-licence, but when the present owner bought the house, it was stipulated that the owners were not allowed to sell alcohol.

The 'Pound' once stood on the other side of the Red Lion, at the fork of the roads to Mixbury and Finmere. This was a walled yard and had a pigsty, small lock-up barn for horses, ponies, sheep, pigs, dogs, or other animals that had strayed and were waiting for their owners to claim them.

<u>Penny Cottage</u> stands on the left side of the Mixbury road, just past the fork to the Bicester Hill road. Originally, it was two, two-up, two-down 18th century cottages, but it was converted into one cottage, sometime after the Evenley Estate Sale in 1938. The previous owner said it used to

Penny Cottage

be a dairy cottage, belonging to Home Farm and that the villagers had the right to walk up the garden and use the water. Now, there is no sign of the water source, pump, or well.

SOUTH SIDE

The Red Lion Public House is an 18th-century building, which was remodelled in the mid 19th century by the Pierreponts of Evenley Hall. Its cast iron windows with octagonal shaped panes are particularly noticeable, as are its tall chimneys of ashlar limestone. A small lane beside the

The Red Lion Public House

Red Lion leads to Nos.40 & 41, two semi-detached bungalows.

On the other side of this lane, heading toward Broad Lane, there was a terrace consisting of three thatched cottages, Nos. 42, 43 and 44, which did not belong to the Evenley Hall Estate. These cottages were built around the late 1800's and were occupied by the local farm workers. To the rear of these cottages there was originally a patio, with fuel storage barns and privies around the periphery. The laundry, then used by the locals, can still be seen, but is no longer in use. It is now enclosed within the rear garden of No. 45 and used for storage. No. 42 did not have access to the main road, only to the patio at the rear, although Nos. 43 and 44 had access to both. Eventually, Brackley R.D.C. purchased these three cottages and in 1969 converted them into two, replacing the thatched roofs with cement tiles, which then became Nos. 42 and 43, with No. 44 disappearing.

The group of four houses Nos.46-49 bear date stones from 1877. They occupy the site of 6 smaller cottages once owned by a Mr Franklin, who sold them to the Parish for £40. In 1831, Franklin, his wife, their 8 children and thirteen other residents of

Evenley emigrated to Quebec. Their passages were paid for by the Parish. The episode was recorded in the records of the Overseers of the Poor. In 1875, Colonel Campbell of Evenley Hall bought the 6 cottages for £40. House prices were obviously more stable in those days! He had them pulled down and replaced with the present houses.

No.47, was a post office in the 1940's, when a stick of bombs was jettisoned from a German aeroplane and fell in the fields behind this row of houses, in the area where a close of modern bungalows now stands. This close is called 'Rudgeway', the name of the field on which the bungalows were built.

No.50. Rose Cottage was originally two cottages, with a passage between, but attached at first floor level. One of the cottages was demolished in 1820 and the present three-storey house was built in its place. Rose Cottage has recently been incorporated into this house and the whole is No.51.

No.52. In the kitchen there was once a stone-flagged floor laid in circles and a fireplace with a large side oven. Within the last fifty years, on the west side of the house, there was an outside staircase leading to a flat or flats at the rear. These were over a coal-yard. The present occupant has received confirmation from the Technical Panel at the Society for the Protection of Ancient Buildings that the house was thatched originally. It appears that No.53 was a later addition but has now been included into No.52. She thinks that a shoemaker, or shoe repairer lived here, as trimmings of shoe leather were found when the broad elm floorboards were removed. The land behind the house, up to and including Rudgeway and the garden of No.51 originally belonged to No.52. There is a barn at the back, which had two stalls and a carriage area and there are signs of previous doors in the stonework, one at the front of the house and one at the side, with a lintel over. This was an entrance to the area beneath the stairs near the fireplace and is thought to be where the coal was stored. As No.52 was thatched and has brick chimneys, it is probably older than the three semi-detached houses to the west built by the Pierreponts, with stone chimneys. One of these houses, No. 58, has a well under the kitchen floor.

CHURCH LANE

From the Green there is a narrow entrance into Church Lane at the North-west corner and on the right, facing west up the lane is Gulliver's Cottage. An 18th Century cottage, similar in style to those of that period on the Green, it has a small extension thought to have been an outbuilding

Gulliver's Cottage

originally. A door of more recent date has been added and is now the front door. Before this, when there were two small cottages, the entrances were at the back.

The cottage was once a pub called the *'Buck's Head'* until 1822, when an Evenley church Vestry minute states that *"At the Vestry held this day (8th Sept. 1822) it was resolved that the Public House called the Buck's Head, kept by Thomas Petty, is a disorderly and disreputable house and that he is an unfit person to be licensed as a publican and that in consequence his certificate should not be argued and it is also the opinion of the persons present that one public house in the village is fully sufficient and that the Honble P.S.Pierrepont be requested to represent this to the magistrates of the district at the ensuing licence day – on the 16th instant.*

Signed: Philip Sidney Pierrepont
Wm Painter   P.J.Hopcroft
Henry Stilgoe   Thos Sherriff
John Boughton   Thos South
James Gamble   Thos Baldwin"

The taproom of the Buck's Head is now the dining room of Gulliver's Cottage. North of the cottage, at right angles to it and divided from it by gardens, stands a thatched roofed, stone-built house of similar date, which used to be called *'The Bothy'*. It is now divided into two cottages, nos. 1 and 2 Boughton

Boughton Terrace

Terrace. From the pitch of the roof of Gulliver's Cottage, it would appear that that it was also thatched at one time. Two more 19th century brick cottages, of a later date, adjoin Nos. 1 and 2 and form a four-cottage terrace.

Footpath to Brackley

From Boughton Terrace, there is a broad, downhill track to a footpath, leading across fields to Brackley. This was once an important route, known in the eighteenth century, as the 'Horse Lane'. Beside it, is College Farm, which formerly belonged to Magdalen College, Oxford. Across the yard, a former barn has been converted into an attractive house, with an old millstone set into the front wall.

The lane swings sharply to the left and on the right is the Manor House, a listed 16th-century limestone and ironstone building, with a distinctive two-storey central gabled porch. After the First World War, it was let as a shooting lodge. This Manor House was the second one in the village,

The Manor House

replacing an earlier one near the Church, which was built in 1232 and owned by Ralph de Evenlee. In 1930, Eleanor Tetley bought the Manor House, which had been empty for three years and was derelict. It had no electricity or water, as the village water supply was pumped by hand. The original staircase was made using two great limbs of trees, steps being fixed where it was easy to fit them. No steps were exactly the same, some being deeper and some higher than others. In 1939, Mrs Cicely Spencer bought the house and lived in it for nearly fifty years.

The lane beyond this point has an intimate character, running between stone walls on either side, with traditional cock-and-hen stone copings and large mature trees overhanging the road. Immediately on the left, there is a glimpse of what is left of the village allotments.

Further along the lane, there are modern two-storey houses, set back on the left-hand side of the road, but it is the mature front gardens of the houses, that have the greatest impact on the lane itself.

On the right, next to the Manor House, but set well back from it and surrounded by large gardens, is Manor Cottage. This was built in the mid 1980's by Mrs Spencer. It is stone-built, with an oak front door and stone lintels over the windows. Inside, the windows are deeply recessed, the walls and corners are rounded in order to make them look old and the fireplace is large and built of brick.

In a short distance, the road takes a further bend to the left, where on the right, there is a private drive leading to Hill Grounds. Peveril's Cottage is on the corner. Hill Grounds is a modern house built in the 1960's. There is an old cottage situated at right angles to it, which is another building that used to be called 'The Bothy'. It was once used by the owners of Evenley Hall as living quarters for their unmarried male servants, presumably to separate them from the female servants who lived in the Hall! The house incorporates, on the eastern side, what were once two open sheds, now the kitchen and study.

Behind Hill Grounds can be seen Evenley Hall, which was destroyed by fire in 1897 and rebuilt in 1898. It stands on a gentle slope in the midst of a park of 228 acres and commands a fine view of the surrounding countryside.

Electricity comes to Evenley

In the early 1930's, the East Midlands Electric Light Company planned to link this part of the country to the electricity grid system and a land line was installed from Northampton, via Buckingham and Brackley, to Evenley. The Church and most of the houses were wired for lighting and cookers were put into the houses of those who wanted them. Out went the paraffin lamps and coal fires, which had been such a feature of everyday life for villagers up to this time. A new way of life had come to stay!

To the north of the Hall, in the fields pastured by sheep, lie two horse graves. On one head stone are carved the words:-

IN MEMORY
ALLIGHORNA
29 FEB
1884

Beyond the bend, on the right-hand side, are four gable ends to barns, which were originally part of the former <u>Middle Farm</u>

Franklin's Yard

beyond. Now called <u>Evenley House</u>, it stands at right angles to the road. The present garage, adjoining the field to the North, was once the laundry for Evenley Hall and had a large drying area. Church Lane terminates at Franklin's Yard, an attractive group of converted and renovated farm buildings, formerly Park Farm. Numbers 30 and 32 formed the original L-shaped farmhouse, whose front door faced the Oxford Road (A43). The oldest part of this dates from the seventeenth century. Number 28 once housed a blacksmith's forge and the dairy. Park Farm has also been known as Road

Renovated Barns

Farm and there is still a footpath leading from the farmhouse to the road, following the line of a much older track. On the opposite side of what was the farmyard, a range of stables and sheds have been converted into cottages (nos. 31-37), while the two houses on the west side replace a large barn which stood there until the site was redeveloped in 1989. Park Farm belonged to the Evenley Hall estate and the estate's working horses were stabled here. The carriage horses were stabled further along Church Lane, at Middle Farm.

Rectory Farm

Returning down Church Lane, a narrow path just after the Church on the right, leads into Church Leys, a Close of 1970's houses and bungalows. To the right of the path, with its entrance facing Church Leys stands Rectory Farmhouse, surrounded by mature trees and shrubs.

Church Leys opens into Broad Lane, the main road into Evenley from the A 43, the dual carriageway linking the M1 and the M40 via Towcester and Brackley.

Lawyers Close is a turning on the right off Broad Lane, as one enters the village from the A 43. It is a Close of 2 and 3 bedroom detached and semi-detached bungalows, built in the mid-1960's.

School Lane is the second turning on the right off Broad Lane and was originally known as Bone Hill. At the top, there are eight 19th century stone, terraced cottages, preceded by three small stone outhouses, which used to be privies. At the other end stand 6 terraced outhouses. The first one, larger than the rest, with an old baker's oven still in situ, was where the villagers bought their bread and took their joints for roasting. A brick addition has three privies facing away from the lane. Two of the other five must also have been privies, as each cottage had its own. Behind the bakery and outhouses are the overgrown remains of a number of pigsties. Back down the lane, the Rudgeway on the right, is a small Close of bungalows and houses. At the end of School Lane, opposite the Village Hall, one turns right along the South side of the Green, back toward the Red Lion Public House.

EVENLEY COMMON

The Common is a piece of land of about 1.75 acres on the east side of Bicester Hill. It was originally one of the plots of ground set aside in the eighteenth century enclosure for digging up stones for road repairs. By the 1980's it was becoming increasingly inaccessible because of the thick undergrowth, and it had been used as a dumping ground for rubbish. The Parish Council decided to apply for a grant to improve it, which meant registering it as a Pocket Park. Work began in 1989 with a party of volunteers who cleared the site. The Common is a pleasant place to walk or sit and enjoy peace and quiet.

CHURCH OF ST GEORGE

The present church is a re-build of a previous church that dated back in one form or another to medieval times.

It was entirely rebuilt circa 1864 with a north aisle, vestry, chancel and spire added.

The previous chancel and nave should have remained intact, but according to contemporary descriptions, the rebuilding was completed with only the old foundation retained. The cruciform plan, therefore, is an authentic medieval feature.

The only medieval furnishing to survive is a timber late medieval screen with central doorway, flanked by cusped lights, which now stands in front of the tower arch. The wooden pulpit was replaced with stone and the tower is surmounted by a shingled spire, a clock with chimes and five bells. It is safe to assume that as many stones as possible from the previous church were incorporated into the new building. An unknown source states that the previous church was recorded in the Domesday Book. It is certain that an unknown benefactor, perhaps a Lord of Evenley , granted the church to the Canons of Huntingdon Priory in c1130, so it was certainly in existence then and may have been built earlier. A little later Pope Eugenius III confirmed the church, with its appendages, to  the Priory of St Mary of Huntingdon, but the donor is not stated.

In a *'dimissio'*, issued in 1344, Evenley, together with the St Mary Magdalene Chapel in Astwick, was listed among the appropriated possessions of Huntingdon Priory.

"Richard Whenman, a merchant of the staple at Calais, bequeathed in his will, the residue of his term in a lease of the parsonage of Evenley from the Prior and convent of Huntingdon to the vicar and churchwardens of Whitney, for the time being, on condition of their paying therout £2.8s.2d yearly in alms to poor men of 60 years of age, of good name and fame and clean of body, who should go to the church of Whitney every day in the year at 7 o'clock in the morning to pray for him and keep his yearly obit and anniverary and say a dirge and mass of requiem". The date of the will is not known, so perhaps the chantry founded in the church by William de Apeltre, in honour of the Blessed Virgin Mary of All Saints in 1333, may have some connection.

After the dissolution of the monasteries, the impropriate rectory and advowson of the vicarage of Evenlai, with glebe and tithes of Astwick and Evenley, were granted (int. al.), in exchange for other estates, to Sir Thomas Pope who, in May following, had licence to alienate them, to Edmund Powell of Sanford in

Oxfordshire and in July following, to Owen Oglethorp, the President of Magdalen, Oxford, by whom, probably on his resignation from the college, they were released in 1555, to the President and Fellows of the college and their successors.

In 1699 all the parish records, which were kept in the Vicarage House, were destroyed by fire.

Interior of St. George's Church

CHURCH HOUSES AND INCUMBENTS

It is quite difficult to trace the exact chronology of the church houses in Evenley and why some are called Vicarages and other Rectories.

The Vicar was the priest in charge of a parish where tithes were not paid to the priest-in-charge but to a person or group other than the priest himself.   In the case of Evenley this was to Huntingdon Priory followed at a later date by Magdalen College.

The "Rector" was the Incumbent of a parish and received all due tithes.   This practice has not been in use for many years but the name of the house he lives in remains the same.

In 1130 the church was granted to the canons of Huntingdon Priory and this was confirmed by Pope Eugenius III in 1147. Therefore from the 12th Century onwards the priest in charge would have been a vicar.

Rectory Farmhouse was built some time in the 16th Century. In 1989 the then owner discovered a Tudor fireplace on the ground floor and on the first floor, in the bathroom, a built in bible cupboard.   This dated from the Elizabethan era when it was enacted that the **vicarage** should be the repository for an English Bible and Foxe's Book of Martyrs.

The house was originally called **Vicarage House** but it is not known why the name was changed and when.   Baker in his History of the Antiquities of Northamptonshire, states that *"in 1542 the 'impropriate'* **Rectory** *and advowson* (right to appoint priest to a parish) *of the* **vicarage** *of Evenley, with glebe and tithes of Astwick and Evenley were granted, in exchange for other estates, to Sir Thomas Pope from whom it was passed through several hands to Owen Oglethorpe the President of Magdalen College and his successors"*

The meaning of impropriate, as in impropriate Rectory, is as follows:-

"The assignment or annexation of an ecclesiastical benefice, (In Evenley's case Huntingdon Priory), to a lay proprietor or corporation.

At the dissolution of the monasteries many appropriated monastic benefices, e.g. Evenley and Astwick, passed into the hands of lay rectors and it became necessary to appoint "perpetual curates" to execute the Spiritual duties of impropriated benefices".

Second Vicarage House

In 1700 the Terrier, an annual list of glebe (church lands and buildings belonging to the Rectory of Evenley and compiled by the Vicar, mentions a house of four bays, the "*vicarage house sometimes called the parsonage.*" In 1730 "*a small vicarage house containing three bays of building with adjoining garden*" is listed as situated on the East side of the church. Fifty three years later, in 1783, the entry reads "*in Evenley one Parsonage House fell down with garden and orchard!*"

Vicarage Cottage is marked on mid 18th Century Magdalen College maps where the carriage drive entered the Rectory Farm Gardens. Perhaps this Vicarage Cottage replaced the Second Vicarage House which fell down in 1783.

The fact that the house by the church is called the 'second' Vicarage House implies that what we now know as Rectory Farmhouse was called **Vicarage House** at that time as it had been from the 12th Century to 16th Century.

The Old Rectory in Broad Lane is a splendid Regency house built in 1834 and is described in the Glebe Terrier of 1853 thus:-

" The note and terrier of all the glebe lands, meadows, gardens, orchards, houses, stock, implements, tenements, portions of tithes, fees, emoluments and other rights belonging to the Parish Church of Evenley in the County of Northampton and Diocese of Peterborough, now in the office and possession of the Reverend John Butler Harrison of the said church taken, made and witnessed according to the old evidence and knowledge of the inhabitants this 20th day of April in the year of our Lord One thousand eight hundred and fifty three.

A Glebe House, built in the year One thousand eight hundred and thirty four, contains on the ground floor three sitting rooms, a kitchen, laundry, larder, pantry and wash house; on the floor above seven bedrooms, a dressing room, store room and two closets - it is built almost entirely of brick covered with cement, a small portion of stone and the whole covered with blue slate - the outbuildings are of stone and consist of a three stall stable, a saddle room and wash house with a granary and hay loft above also covered with slate and are united to the house by a stone walk, the vegetable garden is bounded by stone walls on both sides and on the other by hedges. The Glebe land of Evenley consists of 87 acres and 36 perches viz the " Church Leys" in which stands the house are 8 acres 3 roods 23 perches, in two enclosures and are bounded on the north and west by the estate of the Honourable Phillip Sydney Pierrepont, on the east by the Church yard, on the south by a bye-road belonging to the Parish of Evenley running west".

It is therefore from this date, 20th April 1853 that this new church house became a Rectory and the Vicar a Rector. As the Terrier states:-

all the church lands, tithes and possessions are *"now in the office and possession of the Rev. John Butler Harrison."*

There have been 58 vicars and incumbents who have served the parish and village since the 13th Century and their names are recorded in the porch of the church. Several were only in post for a few years, while others served for many years. Little is known about the majority of them, but there are one or two interesting glimpses of their lives and times which have come down to us.

Thomas Ronson was the vicar in 1560. When he died in 1569, he styled himself the Vicar of Evenley, but specified in his will, that he desired burial in the churchyard of St. Peter's Brackley!

Many were scholars and one, a Roland Searchfield, D.D. (1565-1622) was clearly well connected. After graduating from St. John's College, at the age of 21, he was *"dispensed from the usual exercises, on the grounds that he was engaged in certain duties, at the command of the Archbishop of Canterbury"*. He became Bishop of Bristol, in 1618 and was described at his death as, *"a dissembled Christian, who, like an intemperate patient, (which) can gladly hear his physician discourse on his diet and remedy, but will not endure to observe them"* !

In the early 1600's, several vicars of Evenley resigned their living, although their reasons are not known. One was only in post for 6 months. These may well have been very troubled times for the incumbents.

Since 1800, however, the vicars of Evenley appear to have enjoyed a more settled existence, ministering to the people of the village and the parish at large.